PASTORAL
CARE
AND COUNSELLING

PASTORAL CARE

AND COUNSELLING

A MANUAL

William.K. KAY & PAUL C. WEAVER

FOREWORD BY
CLIVE CALVER

paternoster
press

First published 1997 by Paternoster Press

03 02 01 00 99 98 97   7 6 5 4 3 2 1

Paternoster Press in an imprint of Paternoster Publishing,
P.O. Box 300, Carlisle, Cumbria CA3 0QS

British Library Cataloguing in Publication Data

A catalogue record for this book is available from the British Library.

ISBN 0-85364-784-4

This book is printed using Suffolk New Book paper
which is 100% acid free.

Typeset by WestKey Ltd., Falmouth
Printed in Great Britain by Clays Ltd., Bungay, Suffolk

CONTENTS

Acknowledgements

Too many people to thank by name have helped to make this text what it is. Numerous individuals stand behind the examples and recommendations we cite. Nevertheless we should like to acknowledge the help of Stephen Marshall of Robinsons Solicitors in Ilkeston, Derby, and of Charles Bowler, for their meticulous advice on the duties and powers of church trustees.

The support of family and friends have been invaluable, as have our respective places of work. My thanks (William K. Kay) go to the Principal and Governors of Trinity College, Carmarthen, and to my colleague Revd Professor Leslie J. Francis; my thanks (Paul C. Weaver) go to the members of New Life Church, Scunthorpe, and to fellow members of the Excutive Council, especially to Dr Davids Petts, for their encouragement and support in the writing of this text.

William K. Kay
Paul C. Weaver

Easter 1997

FOREWORD

We live in a world of massive confusion. Uncertainty prevails at every point. As voices are raised in serious enquiry as to what moral foundation, or even spiritual reality, can lie at the heart of the universe, few are prepared to provide an honest answer. A post-modern society insists that experience offers the only valid reality. Each must find their own truth. The only absolute is the absolute that there is no absolute!

The individual is confronted with choice, and personal, ethical or sexual preference offers its own self-validation.

One is left asking the crucial question, '*What on earth can the church say to a world that has rejected the concept of truth?*'

- This black and bizarre scenario confronts us at the end of the 20th century. Yet there is hope –
- hope that the church might rise up to challenge the prevailing view of society
- hope that the truth we offer in Jesus might again be accepted as absolute for all humankind
- hope that individuals do not have to struggle alone, but God himself can walk alongside us
- hope that this world is not an end in itself, but eternity lies ahead of us
- hope that truth can be experienced, and that the church gives encouragement to individuals to find a new way forward.

It is this sense of hope that undergirds this book for which I have the privilege of writing the foreword. If the church is to address these issues and communicate to those who have lost their way, then we all need help in order to do so.

At the cutting edge are those in pastoral ministry – and not just those in professional Christian ministry. A host of housegroup leaders, counsellors, and supportive friends, will all need the kind of wisdom and advice that is given in this valuable book.

Pastoral work should no longer be relegated to the margins of Christian existence. Hurting people need hope – and the encouragement and support offered by pastoral counsel and care can give to many a fresh ray of light which penetrates their personal darkness.

For myself I have experienced the joy of receiving patient guidance and encouragement to move forward in God. Many others have known similar experience, and have come to value the wisdom of trusted friends as they have moved us on in their personal battle with individual hopes and fears.

Yet each of us needs training if we are to be better equipped to care for others. It would be hard to find a more compassionate or careful presentation of the ministry of care and counsel than in this book. May I encourage you to read it in an attitude of prayerful dependence on God, that he might highlight the truth of his love, and the opportunity for us to develop our ministries together before him.

It is my conviction that William Kay and Paul Weaver have provided a major service for the Body of Christ in this book. I believe it should be read widely, and provide a focus for individual development and growth.

If the church of the 21st century is to be different to the church of the 20th century then it must move on this area. The offer of hope is there in Christ, it is our responsibility to make disciples – not by offering rigid rules and regulations, but cautious and careful counsel that each may develop their full potential in God. A church that offers hope, by giving that kind of care and concern, will be relevant for now – and for the future.

Read on – and be blessed.

Rev Clive Calver
Director General, Evangelical Alliance

London, 1997

PREFACE

If you are a Christian, this book will help you. It is written on the assumption that you want to be a fruitful, effective, useful Christian. It will show you how the church may operate to help and support you, how you may learn to overcome your problems and channel your energies. And, if you are sensing a call to Christian service, this book should help you clarify your next steps.

But if you are a Christian minister this book will also help you. It is written on the assumption that you will be part of a local church. You will have a definite role to play within your congregation and, depending on exactly what sort of ministry you have, your role will more or less be concerned with pastoral care. If you are a pastor or a minister whose job description is primarily pastoral, you will be thoroughly involved with people. You will be phoned up and called out at all hours of the day and night. You will be expected to provide words of comfort in times of tragedy, words of congratulation in times of success and words of warning in times of temptation. Your ministry will take in every variety of situation and every variety of person. You will be at your wits' end when problems pile up on your desk and doorstep and when your congregation, despite your best efforts, prefers to worship somewhere else. You will be told your sermons are too long, or not long enough; that your decision-making is too indecisive, or too dictatorial; that you are narrowly biblical in your approach, or not biblical enough; that you should be more sensitive to the Holy Spirit, or that you are far too unpredictable; that you are not very good with children, or that you do not spend enough time on the older members of your congregation; that you should be more supportive of the ministry of women, or that you are a feminist at heart; that your own family is not a good example, or that you are much too strict with your own spouse and children; and you will say, with the apostle Paul, 'who is sufficient for these things?' (2 Cor 2:16).

The book is designed in two sections. Part 1 deals mainly with the minister.

Chapter 1 considers the context of today's church. What sort of world does the average congregation find itself in? How is the world changing and how should the church adapt?

Chapter 2 considers the subject of calling. Are all Christians called by God in some way? And, if they are, how is the minister's calling different? What practical difference, anyway, does the idea of a call make? And how are calling and ordination connected?

Chapter 3 considers the psychological costs of ministry. After all, no one said it would be easy, but what sort of costs are reasonable and what sort of costs are unacceptable? What should the minister expect from his or her family? How is the minister to distinguish between expected pressures and signs of nervous breakdown or burnout?

Chapter 4 considers the pastoral task itself. What is a pastor expected to accomplish in respect of a congregation?

Chapter 5 considers the minister's gifts. To what extent are a minister's gifts natural assets, and how may these be related to the gifts of grace that are given by Christ? What should a minister do if he or she feels unable to work in a particular situation? How do different kinds of ministerial gifts relate to each other and work together in a congregation or set of congregations?

Chapter 6 considers the responsibilities of ministry. What goals and challenges face the minister? How does the minister reconcile the competing claims of family, congregation, vocation and denomination? What shape and priority does the minister's own devotional life have? To what extent are self-discipline and the use of leisure time related? On what principles can a happy family life be built? How can the minister avoid temptations from the opposite sex?

Chapter 7 returns to the local congregation. It approaches questions relating to its structure and the running of a ministry team. It considers matters of leadership and the division of tasks within the congregation. What must the minister do, and what may be delegated? What qualities are necessary in lay ministry? How should administration be organised and how should future plans be communicated? What should happen if church members are involved in obvious wrong-doing?

Chapter 8 targets youth work. What sort of youth group or youth congregation should the minister attempt to build? What approaches and models are available?

Chapter 9 considers the minister's denominational relationships. What sort of priority should be given to activities outside the town and away from the local congregation?

Chapter 10 considers the minister's calling to the city or town. How should a congregation relate to its local community? What patterns of residence determine community life? What are the 'salt' and 'light' functions of the church?

Each of these chapters has a similar structure. It includes a

- bible basis;
- discussion of the biblical text and context;
- set of implications and personal reflections to help the reader apply the texts today.

Part 2 of the book deals entirely with counselling. This part begins with an outline of approaches to counselling, both secular and biblical, and shows how they differ. It places the discussion within a biblical framework. The biblical framework sets the direction of counselling (which is to produce mature Christians) and implies the sorts of diagnoses likely to be most helpful. It embraces the traditional and rich resources of prayer, spiritual discernment and biblical meditation. It rules out the more speculative and humanistic techniques.

Modern psychology offers valuable insights, which are acknowledged and accepted, without providing the whole answer. How, then, should the minister approach bereavement, depression, family problems, low self-esteem, marital difficulties, tensions over sexual orientation? We suggest in a brief conclusion how the information here might be used to work out what to do with fresh problems or by way of preparing people for marriage, baptism and Christian service.

Taken together these two parts deal with pastoral care as a whole. They place the individual in the context of the congregation and the congregation in the context of the world. They are offered to help ministers help congregations, but they will also help non-ministers find a role and come to terms with the pressures and problems of being a Christian and especially a Christian leader today.

Part 1

THE MINISTER

Chapter 1

THE CONTEXT

Bible Basis   *Matthew 16:16–19*
                   Colossians 1:9–12
                   Philippians 2:12–16

The world

The world's population continues to grow at a rate which inevitably changes the old certainties, the old boundaries. But growth and changes take place unevenly and by different means. In the West, particularly in parts of Europe and the United States, the population grows because people live longer, because it is an ageing population. In the developing world, particularly parts of Asia and Africa, it grows because the birth rate exceeds the death rate, because of better health care at the time of birth. Consequently, in different parts of the world congregations will have different age profiles but, within a single country or culture, there will also be differences between inner city and suburban congregations and between long-established and new congregations.

The overall growth in the world's population has been coupled with, and provided pressure for, *technological change*. It is imperative to improve food production and distribution, communications and the availability of services. Government money is poured into these priorities. At the same time, and often without sufficient planning, population growth has led to *urbanisation*: more and more people are living in larger and larger cities. Rural dwellers are decreasing as a proportion of the world's total population. Cities become megacities, sometimes by joining two existing cities and sometimes simply by migration. Nairobi doubled its size between 1970 and 1980 and the projected increase in Mexico City is from 14 million people in 1979 to over 30 million in 2010 (Carter, 1995).

Yet wherever or however the city is built, it tends to erode the traditional structures of family and community. The urban dweller is usually more faceless and rootless than the rural dweller and often less inclined to attend church. The picture of growing cities with large, irreligious populations unsupported by family affection is all too real in the worst cases, though these must be off-set by an appreciation that not all cities are the same. The age and lay-out of housing affects social behaviour, and the kinds of employment provided by an area affect the amenities it is able to provide. There is huge gulf between a new city with separate industrial parks for computer-based jobs and old and decaying tower blocks with nothing but run-down schools and vandalised shops.

The modern city is permeated by the *new technology*. Traffic control, police, security and taxi communications make use of short-wave radio or mobile phones. The post office needs a record of all addresses, the tax authorities need to keep track of earners, the social services need to keep track of all receivers of benefit money and commerce and banking need methods of transferring funds rapidly between individuals and businesses. In essence, and in the big picture, population growth leads to urbanisation and urbanisation only runs efficiently when technological resources are provided.

There are other sides to technology, associated with pleasure and research. The storage and retrieval of information has meant that information about information has expanded. It is possible to obtain detailed computer-generated maps of different parts of the world, to play computer games, and to download the texts of books from the Internet. Moreover home computers routinely handle sets of figures which would have kept armies of mathematicians busy in previous generations; we live in an age of information technology, or IT, and this in itself allows people to relate together in new ways. They may live in cities, but over and above the physical environment, there is an *electronic environment*. Students can meet on an electronic campus. Shopping can take place using virtual reality shopping malls.

This ability to meet electronically allows pressure groups and interest groups to form, dissolve and re-form. Lengthy mailing lists may be bought and sold. New social networks, not dependant on anything other than a computer terminal, allow participants to be part of complex and world-wide social relationships. E-mail, more conveniently than the postal or telephone service, permits like-minded individuals to communicate, swap documents, confer and, if they wish, mount political action. Democracy, ever responsive to such pressures, continually attempts to adapt to such formations as special interest groups press their agendas before politicians. This leads to a climate of *moral relativism*, where one opinion is thought to be as good as another. Particularly in matters of right and wrong, there is a tendency among the young and the educated to believe that nothing is fixed and that everyone has a right to express any view they wish, however selfish it might be. More precisely a study of the values of people in Europe concludes that there is a sharp distinction between the viewpoint of those over 40 years of age and those under. The younger generation is more inclined to be liberal and permissive in outlook; the older generation, which has been disciplined by the hardship of war and recession, is more inclined to traditional views. We have a conflict between a desire for freedom and freedom of expression, and a desire for order, security and morality (Barker, Halman and Vloet, 1992). Similarly, in a large study of 13-15 olds in England and Wales, Francis and Kay (1995: 93, 97) pointed out that 'the overwhelming majority of British teenagers hold liberal views of sexual morality' and that there is a surprisingly large minority (up to a quarter on some issues) willing to break the law.

This relativism is partly accelerated and partly held back by the arrival of new ethnic groups within western countries. These groups very often bring religious convictions belonging to Islam, Hinduism or Buddhism. The result of this is that, after one generation, these religious ideas are often fed into the parent culture. The culture becomes pluralistic, and accepts different world-views, especially religious world views, as being equally valid and these are discussed in the media and explored in the school curriculum. Yet, these immigrant religious often hold socially conservative views about the family with the result that they argue against the relativism of the parent culture. We have a tension that can make some aspects of the message of Christianity easier to communicate and other aspects more difficult.

This tension is expressed in the concept of *post-modernism* which has become important on university campuses. The modern world, it is argued, stemmed from the primacy of reason and a unified approach to philosophical, social and economic problems. The post-modern world implicitly recognises the limitations of reason. It is, instead, a world with fragmented approaches to intellectual and social problems, a world of incompatible ideas which generate irony and cynicism. The post-modern novel may parody modern novels by playing tricks with time and perspective; the post-modern philosopher regards the concept of universal truth as being out of date.

Yet, away from the realm of ideas, the western world, multi-religious and multi-ethnic as it is, finds itself layered into social groups and classes. The expensive world of the comfortable professional contrasts markedly with the poor homes and despair of the unemployed and elderly. The one has private health care, money to spend on foreign travel, credit facilities and opportunities to enjoy the countryside and the arts. The other has a restricted environment and an uphill battle to remain dignified. The 'underclass' composed of people who have been unemployed since leaving school, or without a fixed address since losing a job, are in an even worse condition. They are to be found in the big cities sleeping in hostels or in the open air, and on the margins of criminality (Murray, 1994). An increasingly unprotected countryside echoes these changes. There are now, in Britain, villages where the essential productive and farming life is still the essence of what happens whilst other villages, which may look the same, are really the dormitories of the rich who work in nearby towns and cities (Francis, 1996).

Yet, oddly, despite the financial gulf that exists between the richest and poorest in any society, there is often a common bond between them produced by the same television programmes. The rich in their houses and the poor in their hostels may view the same comedy slots and newscasts, the same soaps and cartoons. They may even drink the same beer and support the same sports teams. At the same time, a greater cultural gulf often exists between the young and the rest of society: the world of clubs and music, of raves and discos, is in its meanings and values quite separate from that of the rest of society. The rich know they have succeeded and the poor know they have failed in the race to material success; but the culture of youth may not recognise that such a race counts: their lives are structured round fast-moving relationships and, quite literally, they move to a different drum beat. They are ripe for political radicalisation and social liberalisation.

Yet underneath the breath-taking major changes *life cycles continue* as before. People marry or cohabit, have and rear children, remain faithful or separate, and die. The underlying rhythm of life remains the same: people are well or ill, and the pattern of life continues, but it continues within a new urban and electronic landscape. And it continues, in western countries, against a general background of family disturbance. The figures vary considerably from country to country, and, even where the family does break up, the variation between socio-economic groups is considerable (Davie, 1994). Two clear trends, though, are observable: there is a growing group of people who have been brought up by a single parent and there are new and complicated family networks based on divorce and remarriage which produce half-brothers and sisters, step parents, step brothers and sisters and distantly related cousins and uncles and aunts.

The church

The previous section outlines the context in which the church is being formed. New church members are likely to hold the views of the prevailing culture, and some of their problems in adapting to Christianity will arise from their inability to reconcile the relativism of society with the expectations of the New Testament. Pastoral care will address this.

The church, in whichever urban environment it finds itself, must be flexible and adaptable. It must overcome modern reluctance to make personal commitments. It must offer itself as the family some people never had. At the same time it must present the right image of itself as modern and aware of technology. A poll carried out by the Evangelical Alliance in Britain showed that 90% of the larger evangelical churches have a computer on the premises and that about two out of five (43%) of ministers have a computer at home (Earwicker, 1996). Growing churches are already coming to grips with new technology.

When we look at research to discover the size of the average congregation, we discover that it varies from country to country and denomination to denomination. The figure of about 80 adults is often taken as a reasonable estimate (Barrett, 1988; Kaldor *et al*, 1994; Brierley, 1991), but this does not exclude much larger congregations and megachurches of several thousand.

Within all these congregations pastoral care takes place at several levels. In terms of the congregation of less than 100, pastoral care is usually in the hands of a single minister, often helped by homegroup leaders or elders or a youth leader or some other recognised person within the congregation. The pastor him or herself will also receive pastoral care at a distance from the denomination or group to which he or she belongs. Our concerns here in this book, though, are anchored at the local level. We have written for the pastor or minister who has responsibility for a congregation, either within a free church context, or within an established or centrally funded denomination, who has to care for people within the normal age range from babyhood to old age. Yet, we are well aware that pastoral care takes place in a wider range of situations than that implied by the local congregation. There are parachurch groups, Christian ministries through Christian institutions dedicated to community care and chaplaincy roles as well as long-term counselling relationships which all require pastoral love and skill. To all these forms of pastoral care, this book is relevant.

The church in the next decade is bound to become more multi-form and multi-ethnic as the congregations of the cities reflect the cities' mixed population. The many environments of the cities will be mirrored in the many shapes of the church. Already, we are seeing churches that run services at different times and in different styles to suit the needs of ethnic communities in London (Kay and Shenton, 1993). Club-style services are laid on for the young, and bible studies for the old – though fortunately each group may go to the services designed for the other. Music adapted to one cultural idiom or another is made the basis for worship to attract one or other sub-culture. The church, in other words, because it already contains and demands a new way of life from its attenders, is foolish to ask new converts to make more life-style changes than are necessary. Dress codes and hair cuts are less important than changes in belief systems and an acceptance of the Lordship of Christ. What the church will offer to many of the highly individualistic young people of the western world, though, is not simply a continuation of youth culture inside the church building, but an ability to appreciate other people – a process of socialisation. If the vice of the young is ageism, the virtue of the church is agelessism. If the young cope with diversity by relativism, the church copes with diversity by understanding and love. If the young immerse themselves in the exclusive culture of drugs and music, the church immerses them in the inclusive culture that finds its focus in the love of Christ.

Questions

1. What are the main advantages to the church of recent cultural changes?
2. What are the main disadvantages to the church of recent cultural changes?
3. Is your congregation adapted to the society in which it is embedded?
4. What traditions and practices does your congregation value which are not related to the society in which it is embedded?

References

Barker, D., Halman, L. and Vloet, A. (1992), *The European Values Study 1981–1990*, London: The European Values Group.

Barrett, D.B. (1987), Global statistics, in S.M. Burgess, G.B. McGee and P.H. Alexander, (eds), *Dictionary of Pentecostal and Charismatic Movements*, Grand Rapids: Regency.

Brierley, P. (1991), *'Christian' England*, London: Marc Europe.

Carter, H. (1995), *Study of Urban Geography*, 4th edn, London: Arnold.

Davie, G. (1994), *Religion in Britain since 1945*, Oxford: Blackwell.

Earwicker, J. (1996), Signs of hope, *Idea*, April–May.

Francis, L.J. (1996), *Church Watch*, London: SPCK.

Francis, L.J. and Kay, W. K. (1995), *Teenage Religion and Values*, Leominster: Gracewing.

Kaldor, P., Bellamy, J., Powell, R., Correy, M. and Castle, K. (1994), *Winds of Change: the experience of church in a changing Australia*, Homebush West: Lancer.

Kay, W.K. and Shenton, W. (1993), *Harvest Now*, Nottingham: Lifestream/Mattersey Hall Publishing.

Murray, C. (1994), *Underclass: the crisis deepens*, London: Institute of Economic Affairs.

"I didn't know I was called to this"

Chapter 2

CALLING

The Christian's Call

Bible Basis   *Romans 1: 1-7*
1 Corinthians 1:2
Galatians 5:13
1 Thessalonians 4:7
1 Peter 2:21

All Christians are called by Christ. It is very easy to assume that only a few Christians have a calling, and that these are called to missionary service or a special and particularly dangerous work which is only open to a few super heroes of the faith. The New Testament paints a quite different picture.

All Christians are called by Christ: to holiness (1 Thess 4:7), freedom (Gal 5:13), peace (Col 3:15), light (1 Pet 2:9) and, if necessary, to suffering (1 Pet 2:21). The point at issue, though, is that the calling is an indispensable part of being a Christian. How, then, is this call to be worked out? What does it mean in practical terms?

> all Christians are called by Christ

Clearly the New Testament Christians, to whom these epistles were addressed, did not all throw away their secular jobs and enter full-time Christian service. They remained, for the most part, doing what they had done before they became Christians, and those who were slaves, at the time when they became Christians, remained as slaves. The calling of Christ did not cancel out social obligations and expectations. The view of Luther and the reformers was that the calling of the Christian should be expressed in secular work (see Atkinson *et al.*, 1995). The Christian was to do his or her work 'wholeheartedly, as if you were serving the Lord' (Eph 6:7).

The outcome of this view of secular work is that it is an opportunity to demonstrate consecration to Christ. It is not 'second best' or a distraction from the real work of the kingdom of God but a means by which the kingdom may be advanced. There may, of course, be questions about the ethics of certain kinds of work. Would we expect a Christian to manufacture weapons or run a casino? There are precise and careful distinctions to draw here and matters of individual conscience that need to be addressed. But in the main, and so far as pastoral care is concerned, it is important for Christians to take a positive attitude towards their secular employment. The most usual difficulty faced by Christians is that their jobs become so vital to the way they define themselves, that they have very little energy left for their families or their local congregations. The job of the Christian minister is to help members of the congregation balance their lives between the competing demands of family, work and church. Too often the minister pressurises talented people to do more than they can reasonably manage because he or she wants to see the congregation progress. It is to the minister's own call that we now turn.

The minister's call

      Bible Basis   *John 1:35-42*
                          Matthew 4:18-22
                          Acts 8:1
                          Acts 9:1-6

The reality of a ministerial call is accepted by nearly all Christian denominations, though they express their understanding of it differently. In most instances the ministerial call stems from the minister's own experience. It is something that comes from inner certainties and convictions, rather than something that comes from external human authority. The biblical data give us models of the ways Christians are called.

In the biblical references, we find two stages. There is a *preparatory period* of time when the disciple is learning about Jesus and his mission. The passage in John 1 shows that two of the disciples of John the Baptist were pointed towards Jesus as 'the Lamb of God'. From John's powerful preaching they would have begun to understand that Jesus, in some way, was going to take away sin.

These two disciples spent time talking with Jesus, and as a result Andrew introduced his brother Simon Peter to Jesus with the words, 'we have found the Messiah'. Clearly, as a result of John the Baptist's words and their own conversation with Jesus, they were able to identify him as the long-awaited Messiah spoken of in the Old Testament. They had theological ideas about Jesus at this point, but no commitment to his mission.

This recognition of the role and identity of Jesus did not lead immediately to a call. It was only later, when the disciples were back in Galilee, and when they were fishing, that they were called. Matthew's Gospel explains that Jesus had by then begun to preach in the area and that he came across Simon Peter and Andrew fishing. In the context of their ordinary employment Jesus said, 'Come, follow me'. This is the *second stage* of the call. It is this personal invitation and command from Jesus that constitutes the heart of the call. The call is authoritative, radical and demands all that the Christian has and can give. Everything changes for the man or woman who accepts the call of Christ. The boats and the livelihood they provided are left behind.

A different, but parallel, example is given in the case of Paul. He had been present during the stoning of Stephen, and is likely to have been aware of the message preached by the early church. Stephen's courtroom defence (Acts 7) shows how the early church understood its situation. Jesus was the Messiah in fulfillment of Old Testament history, and the initial rejection of Jesus by the people of Israel was similar to the rejection experienced by Moses. Whatever Paul knew of the church's preaching, it is clear that he did not come to his Damascus road experience in complete ignorance. These brutal encounters with early Christians acted as a *preparatory stage* to his call.

The revelation of Jesus on the Damascus road was sudden and dramatic and unique to Paul. It was here that Paul understood who Jesus really was. This was effectively the moment from which Paul counted his call.

By comparing the different accounts of the Damascus road experience, it is apparent that Paul not only met Christ there and responded to him personally, but was told in outline what his task would be. Jesus said, 'I will send you far away to the Gentiles' (Acts 22:21). This is parallel to the statement to Simon Peter and Andrew, 'I will make you fishers of men' (Mt. 4:19). In other words the call contains an indication of the task to which the Christian is directed. In essence the call is to a stronger relationship with Christ and to an individualised task.

> the call of Christ is a new beginning

Paul left behind his old friends, values, aims and expectations. For him, as for everyone who accepts it, the call of Christ is a new beginning.

Recognising Christ's Call

Since the call is individual, we respond to God in ways appropriate to our characters and circumstances. In trying to analyse the elements of a call objectively we would expect to find:

- a sense that God is speaking personally to us;
- a desire on our part to serve God;
- overriding circumstance and timings;
- some indication of our general qualification for being called.

All these points can be illustrated from the biblical examples. All the New Testament ministers felt that God was speaking directly to them.

In the case of Andrew there was a clear desire to serve God (which is why he became a disciple of John the Baptist), and the same may be said of Paul who, though he persecuted the church, did so with an intense religious motivation.

In the case of Andrew and Simon Peter, we may be sure that the preaching of John the Baptist, and indeed of Jesus, assured them that the time was right, 'the kingdom of heaven is near' (Mt 3:2). The nearness of the kingdom indicated that other priorities should be put aside. In the case of Paul, circumstances were overriding in a particular way. He fell to the ground (Acts 9:4).

In the case of all three men we are considering, there were qualifications of experience, intellect and character. The hard and disciplined work of the fishermen prepared them for hard and disciplined work as ministers of Jesus Christ. While Paul, sitting at the feet of Gamaliel in

Jerusalem, received a thorough grounding in the Scriptures, over and above that received by most Jews of his day, which prepared him to engage with the full intellectual content of Christian theology.

Ordination

Calling is personal and individual. This calling, though, is to service within the body of Christian believers. It is not a calling to isolation. Consequently, calling is usually linked with a validation through the agency of senior and well-established Christians. The minister is ordained in some way, usually by prayer and the laying on of hands by the bishop, superintendent, overseer or executive committee. Since there is often a lapse of time between the call and the ordination, the call may be tested before it is publicly recognised by the church

> this calling, though, is to service within the body of Christian believers

at large. And, as in the case of the early disciples, the call mày be followed by an intense period of teaching and induction into a new life style before the real working phase of ministry begins.

This basic pattern, stemming from the bible, is followed, with considerable variation, in nearly all Christian denominations (Beasley-Murray, 1993). The emphasis on the personal initiative of Christ is always seen as important, though it is understood more symbolically by denominations which have a less authoritative view of Scripture and the role of the human agent, often the bishop, may be enhanced as a consequence. Whatever the exact steps in the process, the path from call to ministry is well marked and needs to be well understood. It has its own pattern for younger or older ministers.

The young minister

The unmarried person is in the position of being able to ensure that no serious relationship will be undertaken without reference to the call of Christ. For a marriage to work, both parties must appreciate the importance of ministry. If the would-be spouse does not share any sense of vocation, or does not understand the demands that it makes upon a marital relationship, then it is advisable to put an end to thoughts of marriage or to rethink vocation to ministry.

Complications occur if a man or woman feels a call to ministry *after* marriage. Here the spouse has expected one kind of life pattern and finds that the call, if it is followed, imposes quite another pattern. For example the woman who expects her husband to find a steady job and work regular well-paid hours will find herself bitterly unhappy with the results of a sense of ministerial call. The called spouse will begin to sense new priorities and this can produce a deep sense of insecurity in the uncalled spouse. Therefore young ministers must be sure to carry their partners with them into ministry. Without this assurance, the ministry will anyway fail. The danger is that the young minister, in a determination to follow Christ, will brush his or her partner aside and damage the intimate relationship which needs to be maintained in the course of a demanding pastoral ministry.

The older minister

A man or woman may, in mid-life, face a crisis: a business goes bankrupt, redundancy takes place, a marriage breaks down, health gives way or a close relative dies. Something happens which shatters the calm and predictable framework of existence. Often in such circumstances, and because of a deep engagement with God in prayer, the family so hit looks for a new direction and may find it in the service of Christ. People in these circumstances need to adapt to their new lives, and many find this more demanding than they anticipate. While redundancy payments or life insurance may provide the money for retraining, the genuine sense of call is still essential.

What often happens in such situations is that the older minister believes that the skills he or she has learnt in the workplace will be directly transferable to the pulpit and the congregation. In such cases the older minister will often assume that the call of Christ is of secondary importance to general life skills; such an assumption needs to be seriously questioned. The call of Christ is always radical and demands everything we have and, though skills learnt in a secular context will often be valuable, they cannot replace the altogether different basis for life that ministry brings about.

Implications for ministers

First, the call of Christ is an important safeguard against ministerial failure. There are times when the minister feels confronted by adversity and overwhelmed by trouble. When this happens, it is vital to remember the call of Christ. The Christ who called us, will not fail us, especially when our difficulties arise from a faithful discharge of our ministry. Without a strong sense of calling, problems may become insurmountable.

> the call of Christ is an important safeguard against ministerial failure

Second, every minister enters a major decision-making zone occasionally. There are two or more lines of action that might be pursued. Which is the right one? Often it is helpful to think carefully about the original circumstances of a calling to understand the way forward. The call usually contains an implicit direction and entails a number of logical steps for its fulfillment. Paul knew he would eventually go to the Gentiles. Peter knew he would be casting evangelistic nets and catching shoals of people. Without a strong sense of calling, times of decision may become causes of distraction.

Implications for those who feel called to ministry

First, if you feel called to pastoral ministry, you need to find a context in which this can be expressed. The local church is the obvious place where this calling can begin to blossom, but you should beware of trying to force the existing leadership of your church into accepting your ministry. What produces fruit does so naturally.

Second, if you feel called to full-time Christian ministry, then you need to test this calling against the opinion of other Christians in ministry. If the opinion of other Christians confirms your own sense of calling, you are ready to consider the next stage. If the opinion of other Christians contradicts your sense of calling, you need seriously to question the nature of your calling. Perhaps you are being called to serve, but perhaps in a way that you did not at first realise. You would be foolish, however, to discount the opinions of other Christians. They have rarely anything to lose by giving you a candid opinion. You, on the other hand, have a great deal to lose if you mistake your enthusiastic desire to serve Christ for a radical calling to long-term ministry.

Third, if you have an inner sense of calling and this is validated by the opinion of other Christians, you probably need to receive some form of training. In developed countries there is a huge variety of training opportunities available and these run from correspondence courses, to one or two day seminars, to three or four year full-time degree programmes. The longer programmes will certainly make you more versatile and ought to prepare you better for full-time service. The danger of shorter courses is that they will only stress one aspect of Christian ministry and will not equip you for a life-time's work as a minister. Certainly anyone who expects to work as a minister for more than 20 years ought to consider a full-time course. If you try a shorter course and then launch into a ministry without adequate preparation, the danger is that you will do damage to the lives of those to whom you minister as well as to yourself and your family.

Questions

1. If you are a Christian minister, can you write down how you were called to pastoral ministry?
2. If you are not a Christian minister, are there circumstances in your life that lead you to ask whether you are being called to pastoral ministry?

References

Atkinson, D., Field, D.H., O'Donovan, O., Holmes, A.F. (eds) (1995), *New Dictionary of Christian Ethics and Pastoral Theology*, Leicester: Inter-Varsity Press.
Beasley-Murray, P. (ed) (1993), *Anyone for Ordination?* Tunbridge Wells: Marc.

"How can something that is free cost me everything?"

Chapter 3

THE COST OF MINISTRY

Bible Basis   *1 Peter 5:1-7*
                    Luke 14:25-33
                    Acts 14:22
                    2 Timothy 2:3

To make a choice is to exclude a possibility. Every Christian who accepts Christ's call to ministry excludes certain lifestyle possibilities.

In this chapter we have divided the costs associated with ministry, and especially pastoral ministry, into three. There are costs that arise from the nature of the ministry, things that must not be done and things that must be done. There are costs associated with family life and personal finances and there are costs associated with the dynamics of the kingdom of God. These costs, of course, can be off-putting and make Christianity seem very grim, dutiful and miserable. This is not the case because most of the time most ministers would say that there is no better or happier life; but the downside should be acknowledged. In Luke 14:25-33 Jesus points out, in the context of Christian discipleship, that anyone building a tower must first ensure that the cost of all materials can be covered. If the builder fails to do this, the job is half done and should never have been started. The builder is open to ridicule. Christian discipleship, in this respect, is like a building, something that is put together piece by piece for a purpose and is open to ridicule if it is left incomplete. In the same passage, Jesus speaks of a king who is about to go to war and who calculates the size of his army so as to be reasonably sure of victory. If his army is too small, he must sue for peace. In this respect Christian discipleship is like a battle which will take all the resources we can command. It is a battle we can win, but only on the condition that we are fully aware of the commitment required. 'In the same way' Jesus said 'any of you who does not give up everything he has cannot be my disciple' (Lk 14:33).

The nature of ministry

Ministerial work involves standing up to preach in front of a congregation. This act immediately suggests that the preacher is an example, someone whose lifestyle and words should be attended to. We suggest there is a cost attached to being an example. Yet preaching also involves prayer and study and cannot take place without an appointed time when the congregation assembles. The whole life of a minister is for this reason bound by a disciplined framework. We suggest there is a cost in this for the minister. He or she must be prepared for the routine and the time-keeping, for the ordered lifestyle and the different components that make it up.

> Christian discipleship is like a battle which will take all the resources we can command

The apostle Peter wrote, 'To the elders among you, ... be ... *examples* to the flock' (1 Pet 5:1-4). Christian ministers may not wish to act in this capacity, but it is an inevitable consequence of their ministry. Even if pastors see their ministry as having a teaching or evangelistic or managerial emphasis, the power of example reinforces all they do. Consequently pastors will find their faults reflected back to them in church life. They will also, after a while, find their virtues reflected. The generous pastor will begin to produce a generous congregation, the hospitable pastor an hospitable congregation.

The ministerial cost rests in the way example is only copied imperfectly. The minister may have to be *very* hard working to produce a *moderately* hard working congregation. And an extension of this problem arises where there is a disparity between the minister and the congregation in financial security. If the minister gives very generously to church projects, this may not seem like great generosity to the better paid members of the congregation. The minister's contribution may be dwarfed by that of the congregation, and members of the congregation may think that if they do as well as the minister they have done enough. This kind of principle is shown by Paul in 2 Thessalonians 3:7-10. He worked round the clock in Thessalonica (presumably tent making and then selling the produce) to avoid being a financial burden to members of the congregation even though he had a moral right to their financial support. He knew that if he insisted on his right he would undermine one of the crucial lessons he wished to convey. His secular job generated money for spiritual work, and he wanted the Thessalonians to copy this pattern. He knew the temptation to turn paid pastoral work into a kind of aimless socialising. 'We hear that some among you are idle. They are not busy; they are busybodies. Such people we command and urge in the Lord Jesus Christ to settle down and earn the bread they eat' (2 Thess. 3:11,12). The constraints of earning a living would prevent useless meddling while still leaving time for genuine pastoral care.

In other circumstances Paul was content to be financially supported by churches (Acts 18:5; 2 Cor 11:9) and so the situation referred to in Thessalonica was simply to make a point about how Christians should live. Paul's lifestyle was therefore adaptable within the general aims that guided it. What was integral to it, however, was a recognition of the need to speak out, to preach. The New Testament evidence shows Paul to understand his call as being sent 'to preach the Gospel' (1 Cor 1:17) though it also shows that Paul was accused of being an unpolished and contemptible public speaker (2 Cor 10:10). Perhaps he did not find preaching easy but, whether or not this was so, he was certainly effective.

Public speaking is stressful, especially if its success is judged by the level of active congregational response that is not always forthcoming. The trouble here is that, if preaching is an ordeal to the minister, it is likely to be uncomfortable for the congregation. A modicum of nervousness is reasonable, but where the minister is reduced to a stammering wreck or, worse, where the minister disguises nervousness by turning preaching into a few undisciplined and time-wasting thoughts, pastoral life is bound to be an unhappy experience for all concerned. The cost of preaching lies in two directions: first, the minister must be properly prepared, and this can not happen without time and effort. If the minister, as many do, preaches three times a week, there must be a corresponding amount of time planned out and invested to make the preaching effective. Second, preaching must be faithful to the bible, and this means that there are times when what has to be said may be unpopular and uncompromising. 'For the lips of a priest ought to preserve knowledge, and from his mouth men should seek instruction – because he is a messenger of the Lord Almighty. But you have turned

> for the lips of a priest ought to preserve knowledge, and from his mouth men should seek instruction – because he is a messenger of the Lord Almighty

from the way and by your teaching caused many to stumble' (Mal 2:7,8). The words of Malachi apply to modern preachers. They should not 'turn from the way' and cause many to stumble. Instead they should instruct and preserve knowledge. We discuss this in more detail in the next chapter.

The regular pattern to the minister's life can lead to boredom. He or she is on show several times a week and is subject to the expectations of the congregation. After a short while ministerial life can seem frustrating, boxed in, automatic. Yet, within this framework, there are personal conflicts and criticisms. Why is the minister doing things this way and not that? How can personal relationships with members of the congregation be kept in good order if strong personalities want to move in opposite directions? So the classic tension-producing situation for the minister arises when the inflexible routine of the church week or the church year is disturbed by impossible personal demands. A family is in trouble because a teenager is playing truant from school and the minister is called in to try to calm the situation. At the same time there is a sermon to prepare, a meeting to attend or a hole in the church roof. A mother within the congregation has just fallen into post-natal depression and is sharply critical of the minister's failure to pay a visit. When the minister does pay a visit, there is further criticism of the failure to understand the new mother's feelings. There is another service to convene and a sermon to prepare. The minister is emotionally off-balance and the service goes badly. Further criticism follows.

These costs must be paid, and they are paid by digging deep into the minister's spiritual resources. The minister cannot afford to throw away the public pattern of church life because it is on this that the health of the congregation largely depends. So, the minister must continue to preach or convene services despite being unsettled, unhappy and under-prepared. The minister is forced to continue functioning with an unresolved situation and in inner turmoil until, by praying and worshipping (often privately) and meditating on Scripture, equanimity is restored. Only then can an accurate judgement of the condition of the demanding members of the congregation be made and wise remedial action be taken. At some point later the minister's spiritual resources must be renewed, and this is largely a matter of self-discipline, study, prayer and forgiveness, a part of the earlier commitment to the call of Christ.

There is a further cost that is really the opposite side of the fence from those just outlined. Here a young and attractive person needs help. He or she is vulnerable and tearful and grateful for any advice or comfort the minister can give. How much easier, then, to spend time with such a person rather than the demanding and apparently ungrateful parents of the desperate teenager! How much more tempting this situation can become when there are secrets to impart and private consultations to be held. The minister has a duty to help the young person, but places him or herself in danger by so doing. Sexual feelings can be aroused and the minister's spouse can be made jealous. Resisting temptation is emotionally costly – the Scripture speaks of 'bearing' temptation (1 Cor 10:13) - especially when the minister must be tough on him or herself while being forgiving to others.

Family life and personal finances

The minister's work makes demands on the minister's family in ways that must be faced at the outset of pastoral work. Most severe in the short term is the congregation's expectation of the minister's spouse and children. The spouse is cast into a special role within the congregation. If the spouse is a woman, she may be expected to make pastoral visits, give hospitality, convene meetings and engage in a range of public activities simply by virtue of her relationship with her husband. She will often have received no training for this work and she may bitterly

> the minister's work makes demands on the minister's family in ways that must be faced at the outset of pastoral work

resent having to do part of her husband's job just because this is what was done by the previous minister's wife. On the other hand, if the spouse is a man, while these sorts of expectations are less common, he may resent playing second fiddle to his wife and being seen as having no intrinsic value within the congregation. The problem is a two edged one. While the congregation may have unrealistic expectations of the minister's spouse, its members may also feel a right to invade the family home by phone calls at all times of the day or night and by visits for counselling.

The minister (as we shall see later) can take steps to control this sort of invasion, but there is a cost here. The minister can also attempt to protect the spouse from the congregation's subtle and often unreasonable demands, but again there is a cost here. The cost comes from having to disappoint people and from the criticism that may arrive if the situation is mishandled.

And it is a cost sharpened by Jesus's extraordinary words 'if anyone comes to me and does not *hate* his father and mother, his wife and children, his brothers and sisters – yes, even his own life – he cannot be my disciple' (Lk 14:26). Other texts make it clear that a man should love his wife (Eph 5:25) so the word 'hate' must be taken in a comparative sense: in comparison with a love for Christ, all other relationships seem like hatred, they come in second place and without the same compelling imperatives. The tension is expressed by Paul's insight, 'a married man is concerned about the affairs of the world - how he can please his wife ... a married women is concerned about the affairs of the world - how she can please her husband.' And this leads him to the conclusion that someone who marries does right, but someone who remains single does better (1 Cor 7:33,34,38). These apparently competing principles are often resolved by prioritising them. God comes first, the family comes second and the church comes third.

To put the family before the church is difficult when the demands on the minister are extended into prolonged absence from home. Pastors go to conferences, fraternals, sororites and committees. The homebound spouse may be woken late by the returning minister or deprived of company while tedious heckling takes place over the financial crisis in a distant committee. Birthday parties may be spoiled and arrangements for family outings may be jeopardised because business always seems more important than the family's shared leisure. Ministers' children are expected to be more obviously spiritual than others of their age. In short, the minister's family pays an emotional cost for the minister's work.

This cost might be more easily endured if the minister felt well compensated financially. This is rarely the case. Such figures as are available suggest that most ministers are poorly paid, certainly less well paid than they would be if they were employed in a secular job (Brown, 1988). All kinds of implications follow from under payment, some of which have an impact on the minister's family and others upon his or her outlook on life.

The minister's family, at the very worst, may find that birthdays or holidays are not funded to the same level as other people's. It is saddening to see a minister's children with cheap clothes because no other kind can be afforded, and, because children notice these things, the children of ministers may find themselves despised for their unfashionable appearance and resentful of the church or the job which has forced them into such humiliation. The minister's car or holiday may be severely restricted and lead the minister's spouse to try to make up the shortfall in family income by taking on a secular job. If this happens, then the spouse is unable to devote time to the congregation, and the congregation will be deprived of important attention and the minister of necessary support. If the minister's spouse is unable to find a way of making extra money, then the minister may have to look for extra ministerial activities that generate extra pay – it is this motivation that may lead to further absences from home. In any event, the shortage of money in the ministerial home is likely to lead to long hours of work, either by the minister or by the spouse or by both, and this may lead to a neglect of children and their poor performance at school, their delinquency or the loss of Christian faith.

None of these consequences of lack of money is inevitable and we have simply painted a worst case picture. The pressures of finance on ministerial families may be met in some congregations by prosperity gospel teaching, but this should be seen as an extreme answer to an extreme problem. There is bound to be a financial pinch in the ministerial home at some point and this cost should be properly confronted. The ideal solution, in our opinion, is to peg ministerial finance to the pay of an equivalent group within society, say teachers, and to allow ministerial salaries to rise in step with these without annual arguments about settlements. Not all congregations will have the ability to do this, and some may be financially naive and unable to make accurate calculations to account for the different tax allowances that apply or the way ministerial salaries may be buttressed by valid expense claims for travel, lighting or heating. Scripture is very emphatic on ministerial remuneration. 'The elders who direct the affairs of the church well are worthy of double honour, especially those whose work is preaching and teaching. For ... "the worker deserves his wages"' (1 Tim 5:17,18). The phrase 'double honour' certainly includes payment, as is confirmed by the sentence that follows. How much this payment should amount to is not specified, but it must be enough to be honourable. The other side of this equation is given by a text that is rarely expounded. 'If anyone does not provide for his relatives, and especially for his immediate family, he has denied the faith and is worse than an unbeliever' (1 Tim 5:8). If the minister does not provide for his family, and indeed is unable to provide for his family because of underpayment by the church, the minister has effectively denied the faith.

Such considerations place a direct responsibility on the minister and an indirect responsibility on the church. Moreover, though it is common to invoke as an excuse for poor payment of ministers that the ministry is a vocation, this begs a question. What is the vocation to? Vocation simply means 'calling' and the calling of Christ is not a calling to poverty but to service. Thus to say that a minister must be poor because of the calling to ministry is incorrect. It is also sometimes argued that the minister must live a sacrificial life and that lack of payment is a symptom of this. But again this is to miss an important point. Sacrifice involves voluntarily giving away something that you have. If you have no money, you cannot sacrifice it. To sacrifice financially as a Christian is to give money for a godly cause but not to be deprived of money in the first place.

What should happen in churches is not always what does happen, and some of the troubles and costs of ministry arise from bad practice. It is likely the minister will face personal financial pressures of one kind or another, and these must be factored into the general cost of ministry.

> Sacrifice involves voluntarily giving away something that you have. If you have no money, you cannot sacrifice it.

On the other side of the whole important matter of finance is the idolisation of material values, goals and methods within modern society. The minister is able to demonstrate that another way of living is possible, that God and not Mammon is God.

The dynamics of the kingdom of God

Several basic kinds of relationships exist between the church and the society in which it is embedded. This is because societies themselves vary in their hostility or friendliness to the church. In western societies, sociologists have traced a path of development that takes place over generations. The Christian group is at first opposed to normal society and quite distinct from it. After a while the Christian group becomes willing to accept a place within the parent society, for example in conducting weddings and funerals and in other ways marking national events. There then exists a relationship of mutual respect and usefulness. The Christian group serves as the moral voice within society and brings dignity and solemnity to appropriate occasions, but invariably the prophetic and critical voice of the church is silenced. The Christian group supports society; society supports the Christian group. In the first phase the Christian group is called a *sect* and has clear criteria for membership, but when it has a mutually supportive relationship with society it is called a *church* and criteria for membership are blurred (Bruce, 1995).

At times of reformation the relationship between society and church are realigned. The church recovers prophetic fire and campaigns for conversions. In a tolerant society such as exists within the western industrialised world the church is usually seen as one group among many telling people how to live and how to obtain salvation. But, however much society may relativise the church and relegate it to being one group among many, the church cannot afford to see itself in this way. If it did, it would lose its reason for existence and deny many of the claims of the New Testament. Commitment to the church would be almost irrational. So the distinctiveness of the church is essential for its survival and the Christian minister is forced into defending a position that can be depicted as being intolerant or arrogant. In the Sermon on the Mount, Jesus said that the church is the salt of the earth but if it loses its saltiness 'it is no longer good for anything,

> the distinctiveness of the church is essential for its survival

except to be thrown out and trampled by men' (Mt 5:13). In other words, the church must be distinctive, must do the job of salt in the ancient world and prevent corruption, otherwise it is good for nothing and will be downtrodden; it will not survive.

The dynamics of the kingdom of God incorporate these issues. The church is in contact with society, separate from society, critical of society, beneficial to society and preaches about a new and better society where the will of God is done. The minister of the church must in his or her lifestyle and preaching try to exemplify these interlocking and competing demands. There is a cost here. Fashion, ideology and political correctness are critiqued by the church. For example, the preacher stands against pornography and exploitation and, in a democracy, tries to persuade people that some of the activities to which they believe they have rights (for instance drug-taking) are self-destructive, widely harmful and not simply a matter of individual freedom.

There is one further cost within the dynamics of the kingdom that arises from the way Christians are called to live. 'We live by faith' said Paul 'not by sight' (2 Cor 5:7). The entire process of Christian living, whether planning for the future or carrying out daily and predictable tasks, is one built on the basis of faith. Faith in Christ becomes the mainspring for Christian existence. It entails a constant trust in God coupled with a willingness to take what appear to be risks for the sake of God's purposes. 'Without faith it is impossible to please God' says Hebrews 11:6 before giving a long and varied list of many of the things done by faith. Abraham travelled to an unknown destination, made his home in a foreign land and looked forward to a future that seemed highly unlikely to come about: 'a city with foundations whose architect and builder is God'. The list continues showing how Moses was hidden while his life (and presumably that of his parents) was under threat, how Moses himself, by faith, chose the seemingly nonsensical option of life in the wilds of the desert instead of the comforts of an Egyptian palace. Other heroes subdued kingdoms and administered justice. The list inspires emulation and action as well as endurance and bravery. The principle of faith is one that takes men and women in Christian ministry out of the ruts they so easily settle into and puts them in positions where without God's help they cannot survive.

For all these good and sufficient reasons the life of faith is an adventure, but it is an adventure dependant on being close to God and taking risks that are God's risks. Foolhardiness, extravagance, presumption and wishful thinking are not to be mistaken for faith

> the life of faith is an adventure

and the very nature of faith means that it may be questioned by doubt. Is it really God's will that quite so much money must be spent on a new building? Will a new youth club really prosper on this dilapidated housing estate? Or even, more subtly, is all this hymn singing and religious activity leading anywhere – wouldn't I be better off working in a bank? The dynamics of the kingdom of God ensure that all these battles are fought out inside the minister's heart and mind. There is a cost to this lifestyle because the cure to the risks of faith is only to be found in yet more faith. We may think of George Müller whose orphanages sheltered so many youngsters in the nineteenth century and whose reputation only brought him more young people to care for. Faith to care for ten young people was eclipsed by faith to care for twenty, and so on (Bergin, 1905).

Coping with costs

The problems with cost occur somewhere in the middle of a period of ministry. The start is usually launched with good intentions and high hopes. After the honeymoon is over, there may be an expected phase of adjustment. Then, after a few years, the costs hit the minister. It costs more than he or she thought. There seems no way out. Why did no one say it would be like this? One way of coping with these problems is, for a while, to make a point of specialising in those ministerial activities that give pleasure, that make life worthwhile. Perhaps visiting old people gives real satisfaction; perhaps work with schools is a pleasure; perhaps running a committee goes well. Regain a sense of usefulness by performing these ministerial activities and then analyse the costly difficulties that are causing trouble. Clear and sober thinking without exaggeration is needed. If the costs are emotional, then the family must be consulted, though it is important not to place the burden of finance on the shoulders of young people. We know of cases where children, because of their parents' financial difficulties have offered to go without a school dinner, in the touchingly vain hope that this will help. Similarly, if particular people in the congregation are a thorn in the minister's side, it is important not to turn them into hate objects for the minister's family. The minister must share the problem without dumping it on his family. He or she must present the problem as a learning experience because, for the minister's children, this is exactly what it is. They will see how adults face tough decisions and questions and store this attitude away for their own future lives.

The costs of ministry have one advantage that gradually becomes apparent to the minister. They enable him or her to sympathise sincerely with members of the congregation. If the minister walks through life without a care in the world, advice becomes unrealistic, preaching becomes

> The costs of ministry have one advantage that gradually becomes apparent to the minister. They enable him or her to sympathise sincerely with members of the congregation.

detached from everyday sorrows and trials and prayer lacks urgency. Costs anchor the minister in the mudane world so that, like Paul, comfort can be ministered to those who need it with the comfort that God supplies (2 Cor 1:3–7).

In the end some of the costs go away and are met unexpectedly and others the minister learns to live with and accept. God is, after all, faithful.

Conclusion

To the bright-eyed young minister none of these costs seem obstacles to worry about. To the more sober minister all of these costs may seem a ground for pessimism. The true perspective lies somewhere in between. The costs are real and must be examined, calculated and faced. Faith, however, is also real and so are the resources available to the Christian in prayer, through preaching and fellowship and as a result of the ministry of the Holy Spirit. There is no iron guarantee with which the minister can be armed to exempt him or her from the demands of pastoral work, but we conclude this chapter by offering two pieces of advice. First, remember that faith is not making yourself believe against your better judgement something that is untrue: it is believing the truth. Second, there is a 'crown of glory' offered specially to pastors from Jesus himself, the Chief Shepherd (1 Pet 5:4).

 Questions

1. Have you ever seriously considered the costs of Christian ministry? If not, do so now. If so, how accurate was your estimate?
2. Consider an occasion in your life when you feel the cost of Christian ministry was met. Are there lessons you can learn from this?
3. Consider what sort of Christian minister you would be if there had been no costs to pay. What sort of minister would you have been?
4. Who can you talk to about the cost of ministry? Whoever you choose should be sufficiently detached from your situation and sufficiently unemotional to give you good advice.

References

Bergin G.F. (ed) (1905), *Autobiography of George Müller*, London: Publisher Unknown.

Brown, K.D. (1988), *Social History of the Nonconformist Ministry in England and Wales 1800-1930*, Oxford: Oxford University Press.
Bruce, S. (1995), *Religion in Modern Britain*, Oxford: Oxford University Press.

"At least it doesn't look boring"

Chapter 4

THE PASTORAL TASK

Bible Basis   *Ephesians 4:1–16*
Ezekiel 34
James 5:13–16
1 Timothy 3:1–7
Acts 20:17–38

The pastoral task outlined in this chapter is contextualised within the local congregation. Part 2 of this book refers to counselling, which is often amalgamated with the pastoral task, and may be church-related, but is also carried out in other settings. Readers interested solely in counselling should turn to Part 2.

Within the high church tradition sacraments and liturgy are given prominence and some pastoral influence is exercised in this way. The eucharistic liturgy itself, for example, is structured around the reception of the bread and the wine. Prayers, readings and confessions of sin prepare the worshipper for the climax of the service, and the formal prayer book pattern does not vary greatly either week by week or from congregation to congregation. The advantage of this arrangement is that it is possible for communicants to be absorbed in their sense of drawing close to God without being distracted by unexpected diversions or interruptions. The whole service is integrated and the preaching in this tradition follows the lectionary and the church calendar so that Christmas and Easter, as major Christian festivals, are prepared for in the services of the weeks which precede them.

The cycle of the services and formalised confession and intercession within the services is helpful pastorally, especially to those who feel their lives are disordered and lacking in peace.

Within the low church tradition pastoral care is given by individuals with special pastoral responsibility and with varying degrees of emphasis and effectiveness. This chapter explores and expounds a biblical view of pastoral care and suggests that many churches, whether in a high or low church tradition, are falling short of what is desirable.

Structure of pastoral ministry

Within the book of Acts the New Testament presents an account of the emergence of the church from the Jewish community. The early Christian leaders were all Jewish and their expectations of congregational life, and the terminology they used to describe it, all have roots within Judaism.

The synagogue was governed by elders, who were not necessarily literally the oldest men within the congregation, and teaching was given by them or by rabbis who had studied the Scriptures as part of a stage of higher education. Nevertheless visitors were also able to share from the Scriptures (Luke 4:16–20; Acts 13:15), particularly if they were deemed to be rabbis in their own right. The normal day for meeting was the Sabbath (Saturday), but there were ceremonies in the home and rites of passage like circumcision, bar mitzvah, weddings and funerals that might take place partly in the home or partly in the synagogue (Sigal, 1988).

Christian congregations developed with a similar structure. There were elders, regular meetings, expositions of Scripture, and rites of passage like baptism that could have a focus in the home or the church. Yet, the distinction between home and church was less marked within the Christian world because, until well into the second century AD, there were no designated Christian buildings. All the life of the church was conducted in and from the home and, when churches **were** built, they often followed the architecture of the large houses where worship practices had been established (Ferguson, 1987).

The earliest reference to Christian elders occurs in Acts 11:30 where it is clear they functioned alongside the apostles and prophets in the Jerusalem church. Little information is given about the appointment or functioning of these elders, though they are present at the deliberations of the Council of Jerusalem and take part in the decision-making process that sends a letter to the Gentile believers of Antioch, Syria and Cilicia. More light is thrown on the appointment of elders, however, when new churches are formed. Acts 13 and 14 contain a detailed account of the first missionary journey undertaken by Paul and Barnabas. The missionary journey is a success and new congregations are formed in Asia Minor. On the return leg of their journey the apostles appoint elders in each church. This appointment is carried out with prayer and fasting, which underlines the significance of the decision and the spiritual nature of the appointment. The message the apostles leave ringing in the ears of the elders is sober: 'We must go through many hardships to enter the kingdom of God' (Acts 14:22). There is nothing further the apostles can do except trust God and entrust the elders to God; the apostles formally committed the elders 'to the Lord in whom they had put their trust'. This tells us the elders have put their trust in Christ – an act of social, psychological and theological significance – and are sufficiently tough-minded to cope with a church that is likely to have to face opposition.

If criteria for the position of elder remain the same throughout the New Testament period, then the character specification in 1 Timothy 3 applies. This specification is expressed in terms of negatives and positives and in terms of the home, the church and the wider community. The negatives are straightforward. The minister must not be drunk, or violent and quarrelsome, not a lover of money and the husband of only one wife. These characteristics rule out wayward and unstable people. They also show that, in principle, a majority of the congregation is probably eligible for consideration in the role of elder.

The positives are straightforward. The minister must be calm, self-controlled, respectable (with a good reputation in the community outside the church) and hospitable. In many respects these are the opposite of the negatives, but they show how the minister's life demands even-temperedness and a tranquil, sociable disposition. In terms of the home there is the requirement that the family is managed well and that children obey their father. The reason for this is more revealing than at first appears. The family is one of the building blocks of the church. The church is composed of families and is, in many respects, like a family. If the elder is to work effectively in the church there is no better testing ground than immediate domestic relationships. Moreover, the requirement that the elder is hospitable suggests that a proportion of pastoral work may take place within the home.

In terms of the church, the minister must not be a new convert and this also suggests that faith and patterns of life are stabilised. In terms of the wider community, the ministers must be 'above reproach' and

> if the elder is to work effectively in the church there is no better testing ground than immediate domestic relationships

have a 'good reputation'. To these requirements is added one ability that is essential to the pastoral task: this is the ability to teach.[1]

The appointment of elders in Acts is made by apostles or their delegates (as in the case of Titus), but the recognition of modern-day apostles is controversial, or controversial in many denominations. One way of understanding the development of ministry in the period of the early church beyond the book of Acts is to assume that bishops grew out of the roving apostolic role. Bishops were not found till the second century of the Christian era (Lane Fox, 1986) whereas apostles were less common (or even not known at all) at that time. The problem for observing a biblical pattern, or in transferring a biblical pattern to the structure of the church in the 1990s, is that Episcopal denominations do not appoint elders and most non-Episcopal denominations do not recognise apostles.

What is less problematic is the recognition of the ministry of the pastor, often as a single ministry within a congregation. The pastor is recognised on the basis of Ephesians 4 and is assisted by elders whom he or she appoints. Thus pastors take on the apostolic or Episcopal role, even though there may be within their denomination superintendents or presbyteries to whom they are subject. In this kind of congregational structure

> the pastor may be the captain of the team, or the first among equals, but the job of the whole team is the same as it would be if the pastor worked alone

the pastor is part of a team. The pastor may be the captain of the team, or the first among equals, but the job of the whole team is the same as it would be if the pastor worked alone. For this reason, the actual structure of the church is less important than the job that has to be done. Whether there is one pastor assisted by five elders, two pastors in tandem, five elders and no pastor, a minister and a local bishop or a pastor and an apostle (all patterns that occur), the task of pastoring a particular congregation, of shepherding the flock, is identical.

[1.] This has implications for the kind of counselling that a minister may offer. At root this counselling is directive.

The pastoral task

The aim of the pastoral task is summarised as being 'to prepare God's people for works of service, so that the body of Christ may be built up until we all reach unity in the faith and in the knowledge of the Son of God and become mature, attaining to the whole measure of the fullness of Christ' (Eph 4:12,13). This task, though it is an aim and an ideal, is not confined to pastors but is shared by all the ministries outlined in the key Ephesians 4 passage. This means that pastors have to carry out a series of activities, appropriate to their situations, to help bring their congregations nearer to this goal. Pastoral care, though it is a matter of *care*, is also a matter of preparation for action. It empowers and enables God's people, and it operates in harmony with the other ministries given by Christ (e.g. evangelists, prophets and teachers). There should be no disparity or contradiction between the aims of the various ministries. They should certainly not compete with each other or cause confusion in the minds of any particular congregation.

This focus on the long-term and wide-ranging aim of pastors sets their normal daily tasks in perspective. In essence, pastors must look after their congregations as a shepherd looks after sheep. But looking after a church can sometimes seem like painting a bridge – simply a matter of starting at one end and, by the time you have reached the other end, it is necessary to start all over again. In other words pastoral care, without a larger perspective, can seem to be a matter of meeting congregational needs and waiting till new needs arise. The maintenance mentality that can afflict pastors – keeping the church going – must be combated by the intention of 'attaining the whole measure of the fullness of Christ', seeing the church replicate the ministry of Christ himself.

The aims of pastoral work can be considered according to the activities usually used to carry them out. There are three broad categories of pastoral activity: caring for the flock, teaching the flock and managing the flock.

Caring for the flock

This can be understood as the exact opposite of the behaviour of the bad shepherds of Ezekiel 34. The bad shepherds did not strengthen the weak, heal the sick or bind up the injured: they ruled them harshly; they failed to bring back the strays or search for the lost; instead of leading them to pasture, they allowed them to become food for wild animals. In John 10, Jesus, taking up the Old Testament imagery of being a shepherd, points out that it is the hireling, the person who looks after the sheep just for money, who runs away when there is danger and exposes the sheep to predators that scatter the flock.

Each of these activities, taken in turn, unfolds into a series of implications. *Strengthening the weak*, for instance, implies that there are likely to be people within a congregation who are weak. This weakness may be physical or mental or a weakness of faith. If the weakness is physical, the pastor may need to adapt the church building or arrange for transport so that the person concerned can attend the services. If the weakness is so serious that the person concerned is confined indoors, then the pastor may need to co-ordinate welfare agencies who can supply help. In Britain, this may entail phoning the social services, contacting the weak person's family or mobilising church members to try to provide the necessary support system. As the population of the industrialised West ages and as life expectancy increases, the pastoral care of the weak will need to increase. There have been calls for a 'grey' Gospel, a Gospel to the elderly (Evangelical Alliance, 1996), to be preached and such preaching will need to be accompanied by practical action.

If the weakness is mental, then the pastoral problem will be more complex and will probably fall within the realm of professional advice. Mental impairment through various forms of senility affects approximately one tenth of the population over 65 years of age and one quarter of the population over 85 years of age. The burden for caring falls heavily either on the unimpaired spouse or family members who will often value the opinion of a minister or an introduction to the best professional agencies.

> As the population of the industrialised West ages and as life expectancy increases, the pastoral care of the weak will need to increase. There have been calls for a 'grey' Gospel.

If the weakness is spiritual, then Romans 14:1f applies. This instructs the church to 'accept him whose faith is weak, without passing judgement on disputable matters. One man's faith allows him to eat everything, but another man whose faith is weak, eats only vegetables', and each should not look down on the other. In this case the weakness is over matters of conscience. The weak are those whose conscience is upset by eating food that has been sacrificed to idols (1 Cor 8:7). Within the culture of the ancient world the early church found itself in a minority position standing against paganism. Consequently, a great deal of meat was sacrificed in pagan rituals before being sold through the butchers. Some Christians, those Paul describes as weak, were worried that they would be contaminated by this paganised meat. Others took a more robust view and assumed that such meat would not harm them. The possibility for disputes and factions within the church was endless and Paul simply tells each party to respect the other, though he makes it clear where his own judgement lies – it is the weak who are disturbed by eating pagan meat.

Healing the sick and binding up the injured are pastoral activities that go together. The sickness and injury may be physical or psychological. If members of the congregation are physically ill, it is the pastor's job to heal them. This is a bald and uncompromising assertion and needs to be held in tension with other New Testament teaching about the place of suffering in the Christian life. But the evidence of James 5 supports the case for healing. In this passage, Christians are encouraged to pray for the solution of their own troubles, including illness. 'Is any one of you in trouble? He should pray' (Jas 5:13). Clearly, though, pastoral help may be needed here. 'Is any one of you sick? He should call the elders of the church to pray over him and anoint him with oil in the name of the Lord. And the prayer offered in faith will make the sick person well; the Lord will raise him up' (Jas 5:14,15).

All too often Christians are disappointed with the results of their prayers. They pray for those who are ill with no apparent result. Those who are ill get worse, and some die. Christians faced with this kind of tragedy are in no mood for triumphalist faith teaching, and they may well adjust their theology to take account of the complexities of the New Testament. In Hebrews 11:32–37 faith is put into action both in victories and by endurance. The same may be true of modern illness. The position taken in this book is that it is sensible to pray for healing even while acknowledging the possibility that it may not occur. In Daniel 3:16–18, Shadrach, Meshach and Abednego say, 'if we are thrown into the blazing furnace, the God we serve is able to save us from it... but even if he does not...' Their attitude,

> the position taken in this book is that it is sensible to pray for healing even while acknowledging the possibility that it may not occur

in other words, was that God *can* heal, but may not. If we fail to take this attitude, we remove the possibility that God will act directly. If we are forced to use human means for healing, we may still see that God chooses to act in this way. What the Christian must do, then, is to live by faith so that whichever course of action is pursued to deal with a trying situation is open to God.

The procedure for healing those who are ill is laid out in James 5. The ill person should call for the elders of the church (which probably implies that the illness is sufficiently serious to prevent getting out of the house) and the elders should pray 'in the name of the Lord... a prayer offered in faith' and anoint the ill person with oil. How many elders should attend? Should the pastor pray or should all who are present pray? How long should they pray? Should they anoint with oil before or after they pray? How quickly after prayer should the ill person expect to be well? None of these questions is answered by this passage. These are matters which may vary from situation to situation. One matter that is clear, however, is that it is the Christ who heals – 'the Lord will raise him up' – and not the oil.

There is one further clue given by the passage. James concludes, 'Therefore confess your sins to each other and pray for each other so that you may be healed' (Jas 5:16). This does not suggest that Christians are only ill because they sin, but it does suggest that illness will lead to self-examination, repentance and mutual prayer. Why am I ill? Do I need to apologise to someone? Instructions regarding the communion service imply self-examination and self-correction (1 Cor 11:28–32).

If a congregational member's sickness is psychological rather than physical then the pastor may hope that this will be cured by systematic and regular teaching of the Scriptures (discussed in the next section) and the general adjustments and encouragements that can come from the network of relationships that make up the life of the church. More individualised help is given by various forms of counselling.

'Binding up the injured' is what the shepherd would do to a sheep with a broken bone. The binding holds the bones together until the natural healing processes have joined the break. By analogy injured Christians are those who are basically healthy and whose lives have been hurt by an accident. In the course of time they will get better and need nothing more than help or advice in coping with a short-term disability.

We deal with ruling the flock in the section in this chapter on management.

Bringing back strays and searching for the lost is the classic task of the good shepherd. Strays have simply wandered away from the flock and have only gone missing on a temporary basis. Lost sheep are more difficult to track down and cannot find their way home unaided. The pastor must take vigorous and deliberate action to find and rescue these sheep. It is not enough to hope they find their way to the fold or simply to pray that they will turn up one day. On the contrary the shepherd, often to his or her discomfort, must go out to look for the sheep and may face danger in retrieving them. They may have fallen into a gully or become trapped on a ledge. They may be weakened by lack of food and exposure to the cold. The Christian imagination can easily transfer these possibilities to a modern world. There are defenceless young people who have become cut off from the church. Some are homeless and jobless, others are trapped in debt or drugs or crime and still others who, for other reasons, feel unable to return to the congregation to which they once belonged. It is the pastor who must take the initiative in finding them.

Feeding and protecting the flock are vital to any successful pastoral ministry. The shepherd leads the flock to good grassland and fights off marauding animals. In the life of the church the shepherd feeds the flock through the ministry of preaching and teaching. Feeding in the natural world provides a means of growth and energy. The body's metabolic processes turn the food we receive either into the components of tissue and limbs or into the chemical constituents that fuel the heart and other vital organs. If we lack certain foods (e.g. vitamins), certain diseases follow. If, at particular points in physical development we are undernourished, our growth is stunted.

The food provided by the pastor comes from the Scripture. While it is true that Christ himself as the Passover lamb is also viewed as food (Jn 5:55; 1 Cor 5:7), received at Communion, Christ is made known through the Scriptures, and the position of the reformers,

> the food provided by the pastor comes from the Scripture

particularly Calvin, was that preaching and Communion went together (Institutes 4,17,39). Certainly a passage like Hebrews 5:12–6:3 speaks of food in terms of Christian doctrine. 'You need milk, not solid food... Solid food is for the mature... therefore let us leave the elementary teachings about Christ...' The implication is that the milk is the elementary teaching and the solid food more difficult doctrinal substance.

A startling illustration linking the Scriptures to food is given in Ezekiel 3 where the prophet is told to eat a scroll containing the words God wishes to speak to the house of Israel. The prophet eats the apparently indigestible leather only to find it sweet tasting and delicious.

So the pastor feeds the congregation by preaching and teaching. Preaching is one of the glories of the church and every age where Christianity has had an evangelistic impact has been one of great preaching (Allan, 1989). In the early church the apostles preached in the streets of Jerusalem; during the Awakenings on the east coast of the United States, Edwards preached in the churches; in the Methodist revival Wesley and Whitefield

> preaching is one of the glories of the church and every age where Christianity has had an evangelistic impact has been one of great preaching

preached in the open air, sometimes in churchyards or fields; in the ministry of Moody, preaching took place wherever crowds could be systematically gathered; under Billy Graham preaching took place in sporting arenas or football stadia.

The preaching enviroment of the pastor is usually less dramatic and confined to the inside of church buildings. Early on in the course of a ministry, the pastor must decide the extent to which his or her preaching is evangelistic or didactic. The evangelist has the God-given ability to preach the same underlying message again and again without flagging. The message calls people to repentance and faith in Christ. It is the message of the cross. The teacher may preach the Gospel, but will speak on a wider variety of subjects. A pastor whose message is primarily evangelistic will stir a congregation up and constantly present an urgent call to reach those outside the church. A pastor with a teaching emphasis will delight in the details and cross references within Scripture but may lack the cutting edge necessary to evangelise. The first will leave the complexities of the Christian life (for example, what happens when prayer does not seem to be answered?) largely untouched; the second may ignore the pressing need to present the Gospel to the community beyond the church. Both feed the flock, but a balanced flock and a balanced diet require both kinds of emphasis. Pastors may learn to preach in both modes.

Those who have thought seriously about preaching (Spurgeon, 1877/1973; Lloyd-Jones, 1971; Stott, 1982) make a point about the practical conditions necessary for it to be successful. The preacher must be audible, the building or situation where preaching takes place should not be too hot or cold, the preacher should be mentally prepared, able to hold the attention of the congregation, sincere, vivid, vigorous, well organised, able to provide appropriate illustrations, prayerful, not given to off-putting gestures and sensitive to the maturity and capacities of the congregation being addressed. These things apply to all kinds of preaching. But evangelistic preaching, aimed specifically at those who have not made a commitment to Christ, is addressed to those who are not familiar with religious jargon, who may or may not attend church again and whose interests are likely to be firmly committed to their circumstances, their families, work, jobs or schools. Such preaching must show how Christ answers all these situations, and it normally does so bearing in mind that the attention-span of the unbeliever is shorter than the seasoned churchgoer. The evangelistic sermon must be crisp, clear, jargon-free and show that Christ's death on the cross is real and relevant to every listener. Paul says, 'Before your very eyes Jesus Christ was *clearly portrayed* as crucified'; the Greek word means 'being displayed on a placard' (Gal 3:1). Evangelistic preaching gives the listener an opportunity or encouragement to respond personally to Christ.

Teaching the flock

Teaching through preaching speaks to believers about matters of life and faith. It is likely to take place in the context of a communion service or a bible study. It will run alongside one-to-one pastoral care. It will arise out of personal prayer for members within a congregation. It can presume a shared basis of faith that draws worshippers together. This is the normal pattern, but there are instances where evangelistic preaching shades into teaching as when Paul hired the lecture hall of Tyrannus for two years and 'had discussions daily' with those who attended. The Greek word used here suggests a sort of dialogue, a question and answer session, that people could attend and during which they might become Christians. The consequence of Paul's work was that 'all the Jews and Greeks who lived in the province of Asia heard the word of the Lord' (Acts 19:10) and the church at Ephesus was probably influential in founding the other churches in Asia minor – Smyrna, Pergamum, Thyatira, Sardis, Philadelphia and Laodicea (Rev 2 and 3).

Paul's epistles are written examples showing how his teaching worked.

Most of the epistles begin with doctrinal sections relating to the character, plans and purposes of God and move on to ethical matters. For instance Ephesians 1–4:17 is largely doctrinal, while the end of the epistle deals with the way people should live and is divided up to reflect our main sets of personal relationships. The same pattern can be seen in Romans, where from chapter 12 onwards ethical matters are in view. Thus first and foremost Paul concentrated on doctrine and doctrine is supported by both logic and Scripture. For instance, Romans 3 starts with the questions, 'What advantage, then, is there in being a Jew, or what value is there in circumcision?' and continues in a quick-fire way with 'What if some did not have faith? Will their lack of faith nullify God's faithfulness?' which are immediately answered indignantly before giving a quotation from Psalm 51 to stress that God is always truthful.

At other times the questions can come from the church that is being taught. 1 Corinthians 7 turns to 'the matters you wrote about'. Here the Corinthians asked a series of questions about marriage and Paul deals with the matter systematically, first by setting out a general principle (verse 1), then by addressing basic responsibilities in marriage and then by dealing separately with different groups in the church (the married), the unmarried and widows (verse 8) and finally 'the rest' (verse 12). Thus preaching that teaches is likely to be systematic in its approach and careful in its distinctions.

It is also likely to be associated with doctrine, with established Christian truth. It is for this reason that an elder (Titus 1) must be qualified to 'hold firmly to the trustworthy message so that he can encourage others by sound doctrine and refute those who oppose it'. The elder is able to appreciate the intellectual content and implications of doctrine and to marshal Scripture and logic in a coherent way to refute (not simply to deny) those who oppose sound doctrine. Refutation demands a detailed attention to doctrinal claims and an ability to understand them and unpack them. This sort of preaching is not intended primarily to have an emotional appeal. Like anything to do with doctrine, it needs sharp outlines. Yet, in case it is thought that teaching is inevitably hard work and simply grinds away objections to the faith, the example of Apollos who, more than any other character in the book of Acts fits description of a teacher, tells a different story. 1 Corinthians 3:6 speaks of Apollos having 'watered' the young church at Corinth. Paul made the initial planting, but Apollos was able to tend the young shoots like a good gardener by systematically watering them. The teaching ministry, in other words, refreshes the church and helps it to grow.

The protection of the flock so fundamental to pastoral ministry is carried out by teaching Christian doctrine faithfully and without bending it to the fashions and fads of the age. In speaking to the elders at Ephesus, Paul warns them that savage wolves will

> the teaching ministry, in other words, refreshes the church and helps it to grow

come in to ravage the flock. And then he explains that 'men will arise to *distort the truth* in order to draw away disciples after them' (Acts 20:30). The wolves, in other words, ravage the flock by distorting the truth. The consequence of this distortion is that Christians become disciples of untruth and are led into all sort of dangers – they are trapped into cults and their families are kept away from them. 1 Timothy 4:3 presents the scenario of people who will 'abandon the faith' and follow 'hypocritical liars' who 'forbid people to marry and order them to abstain from certain foods'. In the late 20th century, these concerns are still real and fostered by videos, tapes and channels of telecommunication. How often has the pastor found that members of the flock have been given tapes which 'will be a real blessing to you' only to find that there is a fund raising message tacked on to the end of them that is rammed home through dogmatic and unscriptural views on healing or the Second Coming of Christ?

What are the best protections against being deceived oneself? How should the pastor ensure he or she is not led astray? Paul, in speaking to the Ephesian elders, tells them that they should keep watch over themselves. They must measure their own lives, both doctrinally and ethically, against the standards of Scripture. And perhaps it also means that the pastors should keep watch over each other. More personally Jesus, speaking to Peter, and before commanding him to feed the sheep, asked him three times, 'do you love me?' (Jn 21:15f). Peter affirmed his love three times, and it is this love, the love of the individual for Christ, which is the greatest safeguard against error since error invariably attacks and undermines the person and work of Christ.

Yet, when this is said, the pastor must recall what Christian teaching is for. Its primary aim is to produce men and women who are able to serve Christ effectively. All the doctrine, prayer, encouragement, help, preaching and effort is intended to produce Christians who will do the will of God, and do it effectively. In other words, though the church is sometimes seen as a hospital or a school, it exists, like a hospital or a school, for the world outside. Like the hospital it is a place of healing, but it is not a place to live. Like the school it is a place of education, but it is not education for the sake of education; it is education designed to make people more effective in their communication of the unsearchable riches of Christ.

> Yet, when this is said, the pastor must recall what Christian teaching is for. Its primary aim is to produce men and women who are able to serve Christ effectively.

How is this done? One way is by ensuring that, after the preaching and teaching, there is an opportunity to learn by doing, by giving church members opportunities for ministry, often starting with Sunday School and a youth group before graduating to the full congregation.

Managing the flock

This covers a whole range of activities connected with the structure, style, direction, membership and discipline of the flock. We look at these topics in greater detail in chapter 7 and are concerned here to present the theological and ethical basis for management.

First, the responsibilities of management are not carried lightly. The pastor is accountable to God for the state of the congregation (1 Thess 5:13) and receives authority from God to enable these responsibilities to be successfully discharged. The balance between authority and responsibility and between authority and compassion is not always easy to strike, but is perfectly exemplified in the ministry of Christ himself to whom pastors should always look. There are times when the pastor must lovingly rebuke a member of the church (usually in private at first) and others when the remedy is to be found in prayer and encouragement. Situations will vary, and no simple rule will cover all cases. Certainly pastoral authority should never be used to damage the flock and pastors who, because they feel threatened or stressed, overreact by constantly asserting their own powers may be tempted to act dictatorially. In such instances it is important to emphasise that the authority of the Christian pastor is based on a willingness to serve as well as upon the God-given pastoral role. Peter finds it necessary to remind Christian pastors not to 'lord it over' their flocks but rather to be clothed with humility, a warning which would not have been issued if pastors could always be relied upon to keep the right attitude to the people in their care (1 Pet 5:3,5).

Second, the managing or ruling functions of the pastor are associated with the same functions in the family. 'If anyone does not know how to manage his own family, how can he take care of God's church' (1 Tim 3:5). So one way of asking how the pastoral management should be understood is to ask the same question about families and then to draw parallels. The management of the family operates on several levels. There are emotional needs, financial requirements, competing interests and long-term hopes. Anyone managing a family discovers very quickly that children squabble, adults can disagree and people are happiest when they like doing what is expected of them. Management, at this point, is a matter of priorities. Emotional storms must be quieted before consensus can be reached. The consensus may revolve around the needs of a particular member of the family (someone has broken a leg, someone is elderly and alone) or the financial requirements of other members of a family (someone is getting married, someone is going on a school trip). Or there may be competing interests: one person needs sleep and another needs to practise a musical instrument. Long-term hopes (saving for the future) may be balanced against short-term wishes (a piece of household machinery is broken). And the same sorts of issues must be faced within the church. Emotional storms may blow up, financial pressures may build up and interests may compete (should church resources be given to one favoured project or another?). Pastors need the same skills and self-control as parents to reach satisfactory solutions. They also need a relationship with their flock which is, in some sense, like that of parents with family members.

> management is a matter of priorities

The ethical basis of pastoring rests on relationships. It might be argued that pastoring is founded on abstract theological principles: God calls men and women to be pastors and others to be sheep; he gives pastors rights over the lives of others, and congregational members duties to recognise those rights. But we would argue that this is to misperceive the nature of pastoring. The pastor knows the sheep personally, and they know the pastor. The sheep trust the pastor, and the pastor trusts God who is the pastor's pastor. The personal nature of pastoring ensures that abstract principles are less important than human qualities. Or, to put this another way, the great commands, said Jesus, were to love God and to love neighbour and this love is, at its least, expressed by doing for others what you would wish them to do for you. The pastor treats the sheep as he would want to be treated if he were in their position, and vice versa. This is one reason why the managing function of the pastor is like that of the parent. The parent is expected to display 'natural affection' and to love children. If this were not so, then the ultimate parental relationship expressed by that between the Father and the Son would have no exemplary value. Thus we argue that the ethical basis of pastoring is not a form of legalism but a form of love.

How can the pastor expect to be sufficient for all these considerations? It is to the gifts of the pastor we now turn.

Questions

1. If you are a Christian minister, list the pastoral tasks you find hardest to carry out. What are the reasons for these difficulties? Now list the tasks you find easiest. Again, what are the reasons for this?
2. What aspects of your Christian tradition are least in line with a biblical account of the tasks of the pastor?
3. Give two examples of the pastoral ministry of Christ within the Gospels.

References

Allan, J.D. (1989), *The Evangelicals: the Story of a Great Christian Movement*, Exeter: The Paternoster Press.

Calvin, J. (1559/1960), *Institutes of the Christian Religion*, Philadelphia: The Westminster Press.

Evangelical Alliance (1986), *Idea* (September–October).

Ferguson, E. (1987), *Backgrounds of Early Christianity*, Grand Rapids: Eerdmans.

Lane Fox, R. (1986), *Pagans and Christians*, Harmondsworth: Penguin.

Lloyd-Jones, M. (1971), *Preachers and Preaching*, London: Hodder and Stoughton.

Sigal, P. (1988), *Judaism: the evolution of a faith*, Grand Rapids: Eerdmans/Paternoster.

Spurgeon, C.H. (1887/1973), *Lectures to My Students*, London: Marshall, Morgan and Scott.

Stott, J.R.W. (1981), *I Believe in Preaching*, London: Hodder and Stoughton.

"Thanks, I certainly prefer useful gifts"

Chapter 5

THE MINISTER'S GIFTING

Bible Basis   *1 Timothy 3:1-12*
1 Corinthians 12:1-11
Romans 12:3-8
Ephesians 4:1-12

The call of Christ imposes an urgency on the individual's life. There is something that must be done, a task, or a series of tasks, that override normal priorities. It is for this reason that men and women who feel called by Christ are prepared to cross oceans, stand up against fashions and risk their lives with unpopular opinions. To carry forward the tasks and the call, the individual needs a character that will not buckle under strain. Of John the Baptist, Jesus asked rhetorically, 'What did you go out into the desert to see? A reed shaken by the wind?' (Mt 11:7). John was no weedy reed, but a preacher whose uncompromising preaching led him to jail and death.

In almost any field of human achievement character is important, perhaps more important than gift. Character ensures stability, overcomes obstacles and temptation and is the vehicle that carries a gift to its mature success. It is no surprise, then, as we saw in the previous chapter, that the main qualifications for a Christian leader given in the pastoral epis-

> character ensures stability, overcomes obstacles and temptation and is the vehicle that carries a gift to its mature success

tles focus on character requirements. These are the fundamental necessities for any Christian ministry, including pastoral ministry.

The biblical description of human beings is distinctive and unique. It owes nothing to other religions or to theories of modern psychology. Genesis 1–3 shows human beings made in the image of God – special, rational, able to relate to God, able to talk, plan, rule over nature, remember, and composed of both a physical body and an immaterial soul. The Genesis passage also shows human beings capable of disobeying God and being cut off from divine blessing and degenerating into deceit, murder and arrogance. The human body remains alive, but the spiritual part is alienated from God and craves an alternative object of worship, usually the image of an animal.

In a compressed account of human history the Epistle to the Romans interprets and explains subsequent events. Divine law was given to the Jewish people through the ministry of Moses. Those who embraced this law received a complete set of commands by which their lives were regulated. They were able to understand God's will in detail and, when they sinned, they were able to offer sacrifices of various kinds that brought them back into fellowship with God. But this law dealt with externals, with actions and behaviours, and not with the inner life of the mind and the affections. The old covenant that accompanied this law was replaced by a new covenant made by Jesus Christ. Announcement of this new covenant, and a partial description of it, is found in the prophetic writings of the Old Testament, '"The time is coming", declares the Lord, "when I will make a new covenant with the house of Israel... I will put my law in their minds and write it on their hearts"' (Jer 31:31,33).

The new covenant is inward in its effects. Jesus, in contrasting his teaching with the old covenant, says, 'You have heard that it was said to people long ago [in the old covenant], "Do not murder"... but I tell you that anyone who is angry with his brother will be subject to judgement... you have heard that it was said [in the old covenant] "Do not commit adultery". But I tell you that anyone who looks at a woman lustfully has already committed adultery with her in his heart' (Mt 5:21–30). The teaching of the old covenant concerned the outward act. The teaching of Jesus concerned the inward thought. If the inward thought is pure, the outward act has no chance of being committed. This line of teaching is applied vigorously to the Pharisees whose obsessions with external ritual led them to ignore attitudes of heart. Jesus said to them, 'You clean the outside of the cup and dish, but inside they are full of greed and self-indulgence' (Mt 23:25).

How is this inward transformation to be achieved? The New Testament has several ways of describing the process. It says of the Gentiles that their 'hearts were purified by faith' (Acts 15:9). Jesus tells the Jewish religious leader Nicodemus, who lived according to the Mosaic law, that he must 'be born again' or 'born from above' (Jn 3:3). Paul, speaking of his own experience, recounts how he tried desperately to keep the Mosaic law and failed. 'I found the very commandment that was intended to bring life actually brought death' because 'I would not have known what coveting really was if the law had not said, "do not covet"' and he continues 'for I have desired to do what is good, but I cannot carry it out' (Rom 7). This state of affairs, of wanting to do good but being unable to carry it out, of feeling the frustrating effect of sin, is resolved only and completely by the power of Christ. It is Christ's death that enables the believer to be justified and freed from the guilt of sin. 'This righteousness from God comes through faith in Jesus Christ to all who believe' because 'God presented him as a sacrifice of atonement' (Rom 3:22–25). After justification, Paul is able to explain how a new lifestyle emerges. The old life is dead and the Spirit of God, within the believer, operates to change habits, affections and motivations to produce a new character.

There are also two simpler models of the human psyche presented in the bible. The believer is like a vessel into which liquid is poured. The vessel must be clean so that what is poured in is the same as what is poured out. The Christian is the vessel and has a duty to be clean, and God fills the vessel with whatever is necessary for a situation or occasion (Rom 9; 2 Cor 4; 1 Thess 4:4; 2 Tim 2:21). The other model is of the Christian as a tree that bears fruit (Mt 7:17; Ps 1). Here the product of the Christian life is found in fruit that grows from the tree which reflects the inner nature of the tree. Good trees produce good fruit. Fruit reflects **the inner life of the Christian is vital to its outward product** the kind of tree on which it grows – apples on apple trees, and so on. The two models concur in saying that the inner life of the Christian is vital to its outward product.

If we put these models and explanations together we end up with a comprehensive account of Christian responsibility in respect of character. The Christian believes in the merits of Christ's death and experiences the active help of the Holy Spirit in breaking free from sin. There will be a struggle here, as there was for Paul, because the formation of new habits of thought and action can only occur if the believer really wants this. This is the first place where the responsibility rests – in the will. Afterwards the Christian has a responsibility to remain clean and rooted in Scripture and, if this is done, God's work will flow or grow from within.

Gifts to people

In the modern world a gift requires a giver and a receiver, and the receiver must appreciate that the gift is being offered in order to take it. Once the gift has been given it belongs to the receiver rather than the giver.

The modern idea of a gift is exactly the same as the New Testament idea. So when the New Testament speaks of gifts, it refers to possessions which God offers and which may be appropriated by Christians.

As a result of their biological inheritance people vary in their capacities and abilities. No one would claim that Mozart's music or Picasso's art were anything other than as a consequence of innate capabilities. But, exceptional though these two men were, they illustrate a general principle. People are born with capabilities they can develop and use. Christians who see the entire process of life from conception onwards as being under the care of God have no problem in assuming that what are sometimes called 'natural gifts' are built-in by God's goodness. These gifts are bedded within the individual's personality and enhanced or developed by upbringing and education. They are most obviously seen in musical or mathematical abilities and an individual's whole life may be shaped by their usage.

But, in addition to the purely human capabilities which individuals possess, and which may or may not be consecrated to the work of Christ, are *charismata*. The Greek word for 'grace' is *charis* and the word *charisma* (plural *charismata*) is closely linked with it. The *charismata* are gifts that express the grace of God in an individual and, in the New

Testament, they are associated either with Christ or with the Holy Spirit. For example, Romans 6:23 says that 'the gift (*charisma*) of God is eternal life through Jesus Christ our Lord'. Eternal life, as a gift, is intimately linked with Christ. On the other hand, the *charismata* of 1 Corinthians 12 are intimately linked with the Holy Spirit.

Such gifts are extremely varied and the three places in the New Testament where they are most fully listed are Romans 12, 1 Corinthians 12 and 1 Peter 4. Both passages are dealing with the church rather than with individual competence, but this is because the gifts given to individual Christians are designed to help the church and are not simply for private gratification or glorification.

The list in Romans 12:6–8 is:

- prophecy
- serving
- teaching
- encouraging
- contributing to the needs of others
- leadership and
- showing mercy

The list in 1 Corinthians 12:8–10 is:

- wisdom
- knowledge
- faith
- gifts of healing
- miraculous powers
- prophecy
- ability to distinguish between spirits
- ability to speak with different kinds of tongues (languages)
- interpretation of tongues (languages)

1 Peter 4:9–11 is set out differently. It mentions:

- hospitality
- speaking
- serving

The lists obviously overlap in two respects. First, they refer to speaking – verbal communication – whether in prophecy, ability to speak in tongues or to interpret tongues. This is what we would expect since the Holy Spirit is associated with speech throughout the bible and words are the vital currency of human thought and culture. Second, the lists imply recognised Christian ministries. Both include prophecy (with its counterpart of Christian prophet), and the first includes teaching and the second knowledge and wisdom (with the counterpart of the Christian teacher). In this way, the lists of gifts are connected to the list of ministries in Ephesians 4.

How are human beings to receive gifts from God? The answer here must fit the teaching of the bible as a whole. Everything human beings have from God is through grace. In other words, even though the new covenant is a covenant where gifts abound, gifts remain gifts – provided by the unmerited favour of God. But this does not appear to take us much further forward unless these gifts are being offered by God all the time. And this, indeed, is what is happening. Most Christians believe that God offers his saving power all the time – that it is not switched on and off arbitrarily – and that when human beings turn to God in repentance and faith that God will hear them. There may be arguments among Christians about how and when human beings turn to God in repentance and faith, but this is quite separate from what happens when human beings actually do so. In the same way, the gifts of God are permanently offered.

This is not to say that any individual can decide, without further ado, that he or she will take all the *charismata* necessary to become, for example, an evangelist. The text of 1 Corinthians 12:11 is quite clear on this matter. The gifts are given by the Holy Spirit, but they are given as the Spirit wills, and this implies that there is nothing automatic happening here. Other parts of the New Testament, however, give Christians confidence to ask God for gifts and to expect that the Holy Spirit will be given to them, and it is for this reason that we expect the gifts to become active in Christian lives as a result of prayer. The first part of Luke 11 is concerned entirely with prayer and the second gives a parable or illustration of a son asking a father for various foods, which the father naturally gives. If the earthly father gives food, 'how much more will your Father in heaven give the Holy Spirit to those who ask him!' declares Jesus. By analogy, then, we would expect Christians to receive gifts to do God's work, provided that they pray for them.

There are two passages in the epistles supporting this approach. The first concerns interpretation of tongues. 'Anyone who speaks in a tongue should pray that he may interpret' (1 Cor 14:13). Since speaking with tongues is primarily of benefit to the individual (1 Cor 14:1–5), prayer for the ability to interpret tongues is unselfish and may be made confidently. And it does not take a great extension of this principle to assume that prayer for other *charismata* may be equally legitimate. After all, interpretation is simply listed along with the other gifts earlier in the same epistle. There is no indication that it should be treated any differently from the other gifts or that the general guidelines regarding spiritual gifts treat one as different from the rest. So we conclude that one way pastors may extend their repertoire of gifts is by prayer. This is confirmed by the passage in James 1:5 where 'if any of you lacks wisdom, he should ask God who gives generously to all without finding fault, and it will be given to him'. Again, the Christian should ask God, or pray, for what he or she lacks. But the connection with *charismata* exists because one of the gifts listed in 1 Corinthians 12 is wisdom. It would be strange if the offer of wisdom in James 1 were in some way different, or on a different basis, from the kind of wisdom being discussed in 1 Corinthians. There is, surely, only one kind of Christian wisdom.

The wider consideration of gifts is relevant to all Christians wherever they may worship and in whatever country they may live. The narrower application of the subject leads to the question about the gifts appropriate to the pastor. Are there some gifts that all pastors need and without which they cannot be pastors? Are there some gifts that people recognise themselves to have and which lead them to realise that they are called to be pastors?

The only way to answer these questions is to compare the tasks of the pastor with the gifts listed in the New Testament. The table below (using the tasks in chapter 4) does this.

Task	Gift
prepare God's people for works of service	teaching prophecy wisdom

build up the body of Christ	teaching
	encouraging
	serving
	contributing to the needs
	  of others
	leadership
	faith
	ability to distinguish
	  between spirits
	interpretation of tongues
	hospitality

strengthen the weak	encouraging
heal the sick or bind up the injured	healing miraculous powers
bring back the strays or search for the lost	showing mercy
feed the sheep	teaching
protect the sheep	faith teaching
rule	wisdom

There are some gifts that match more than one task. For example, teaching or wisdom might apply to nearly all the pastoral tasks in one way or another. For this reason, as well as on the grounds given in 1 Timothy 3:2, a pastor must be able to teach. Without this ability, there is no beginning to this ministry, at least not in its fullest form. Pastoral care for the weak may be offered by any member of a congregation who has the ability to encourage, but a recognised pastor, with responsibility for a congregation, cannot function without an ability to teach.

So, can someone who is unable to teach learn to teach? Can they be gifted to teach? The answer to this must be 'yes', but experience suggests a proviso. Teaching, though it is a *charisma*, is also a natural ability. If this were not so, then only those who were Christians would be able to teach. So the teaching *charisma* must be harmonious with an underlying natural ability. If a Christian does have teaching ability, he or she may or may not be called to pastoral work; this depends on the basic call of Christ to the individual.

In the hustle and bustle of pastoral life the most likely gifts the pastor will need are those of wisdom, faith, healing the sick, leadership and prophecy. These gifts may certainly be made the subject of prayer, but it would be misleading to think that a Christian who had received wisdom to solve a particular problem could also solve every other problem. In other words the gifts are specific to particular situations. Faith is needed on lots of occasions and leadership will not cover every possibility. Experience suggests that some Christians find it easier to believe God for one kind of provision rather than another. The faith of George Müller for the orphans in his care grew from his own relationship with God. Other Christians might find it easier to believe God for success in an evangelistic crusade or for healing or for money for a building. Faith, in each case, is the same substance, and it is faith in the same God, but the outcome of the faith varies. There is a real sense, then, that the gifts God gives are constantly renewed and constantly reapplied.

Gifts of people

We have spoken of gifts, whether natural or charismatic, being given to Christians by God. But there is another perspective on this matter. The Christian may be given as a gift by God to the church or a special section of the church. When this happens the Christian, surrendered to God, is given with all his or her faults and failings, gifts and experiences, to the church. In short, the gift is the gifted person. This should not be a surprise because God 'gave' his Son for the sin of the world (Jn 3:16) and Jesus said to the apostles, 'As the Father has sent me, I am sending you' (Jn 20:21). The texts show that 'giving' and 'sending' correspond: to be sent is to be given.

Ephesians 4 takes up the theme and shows Christ giving ministers of various kinds to the church. There are four or five kinds of ministry to the church. These are apostles, prophets, evangelists and pastors/teachers or pastors *and* teachers. In other words all the pastors may also be teachers, but teachers may also exist as a separate ministry without additional pastoral responsibility. In practical terms, this distinction makes no difference to pastoral care. But it does make a difference to the way the pastor views his or her ministry.

It reminds the pastor that his or her ministry is initiated by Christ. This is a truth the pastor must cling on to. Too easily the pastor can slip into feeling like the secular employee of a voluntary organisation or, worse, an employee of an unenlightened congregation with no resources and no plans to change. The 'givenness' of the pastor may lead into some strange places – for Paul into prison and to shipwrecks and eventually to Caesar – and for most pastors to less dangerous locations but places that lie within the providence of God.

Gifts in action

Jesus was a great deal more practical than detractors of Christianity suppose. 'By their fruits' he said 'you will know them' (Mt 7:17). On another occasion, when he was being criticised for not being ascetic enough, he rounded on his critics and said, 'Wisdom is proved right by her actions' (Mt 11:19). The real pastor will be recognisable by results that need no advertising or hype. There will be a well-cared for congregation that is active and strong.

A congregation can immediately feel the impact of gaining or losing a real pastor. An elderly couple looked after a congregation in a university town. They welcomed the young students and took trouble to make them feel at home. They learnt their names, provided appropriate social and spiritual activities and ensured the teaching given in the church was helpful to the young as well as the old. Then the old pastor died and for a while his wife helped to exercise a pastoral ministry. Eventually she grew unwell and the church was taken over by a woman who considered herself to be a prophet. She was a dominant individual and perpetually preached apocalyptic sermons which she seemed to collect from transatlantic tapes and videos. The congregation were told almost every Sunday that they must submit to the new leadership since this is what God required. Most of the students left. Those who remained were offered no opportunity to participate in church life. The consequence of this sad story is that Christian young people who had grown up in a Christian family and been nurtured in their own churches were presented with more reasons for leaving the Christian faith than they were for remaining in it. Such are the dangers for a congregation headed by so-called prophets.

> a congregation can immediately feel the impact of gaining or losing a real pastor

From the point of view of the minister who has a pastoral ministry, settling in to the tasks should seem comfortable. There should be a fit between person and work such that the work feels right. A man who was catapulted into pastoral ministry (wrongly as it turned out) began to prepare his teaching and preaching. He worked all day to produce a sermon and the time came in the evening when he was to give it. He preached and the congregation listened politely. He felt inadequate. The next time he preached, he spent even longer preparing his sermon. Again, there was polite attention, but he felt his congregation were not interested in what he had to say. Truth to tell, he was not interested in what he had to say. The next time he was to preach he put off the tedious hours of preparation. He got up early and read the passage from the bible he was to speak from. The sermon was no better or worse than the others. He grew depressed. He lapsed morally. He eventually left the ministry. In this case the problems were highlighted by the existence of other people in the congregation who preached from time to time. With less time to prepare, they preached effectively and easily and earned the respect and favour of the congregation. The pastoral gift, of course, is not only a matter of preaching, but it is a crucial part of it. The real pastor, out of study and prayer, will be able to say something appropriate to the people in his or her care.

One of the problems the pastor faces, especially in busy and demanding times, is that of feeling 'burnt-out', of having constantly 'given out' to others to the extent that there seems nothing left to give. The burnt-out pastor can become callous and bored by other people's troubles, less patient and less willing to help. The pastoral gift is still intact and the pastor is still a gift to the congregation, but the enthusiasm has gone. The extent of burnout has been studied (Francis and Jones, 1996). Some of the clergy concerned work a sixty hour week and the data indicate that they worry and are tense more than other clergy. The burnt-out clergy are likely to be hyperactive and to sleep badly. They may feel stress in their marriages. They often feel a sense of powerlessness when confronted

the extent of burnout has been studied

with intractable situations or church members. The remedy for this state of affairs, once it has been diagnosed, is largely a matter of common sense. The burnt-out clergy need to rest, meditate, take steps to increase their general level of fitness and reorganise their work load. They also need input from other ministry.

A whole network of support for ministers must be found. There are three places where this may be established. First, the minister may find in his or her own experience with God, there is renewal and recharging. Fasting and

a whole network of support for ministers must be found

prayer, or retreat and study can provide the necessary refreshment. To find this help, considerable time and self-discipline is necessary but, in practice, few pastors seem to have the determination to pursue this course. Second, the minister may find help through association with other ministers. If this association is to be effective, it is necessary for the burnt-out pastor, or even the pastor whose resources are depleted, to admit his or her difficulties to the peer group. As a matter of pride, this is a humbling admission to make. Why should my situation be so hard, my parish so demanding, that I need to go crying on the shoulders of others? Is there something wrong with me? Am I really called to the ministry? The questions come tumbling out and are not easily put into perspective. Third, the minister may find that, as a result of the ministry given over some years, that there is help and fellowship within the church: the minister begins to reap some of the encouragement he or she has sown. The church begins to give back to the minister what it has received.

Finally, the gifts any pastor customarily uses may be expected to grow or change during the course of a ministerial life. At the start of a ministry, the pastor, without any experience but with plenty of energy, may be keen to start a children's work and devote time into running this or training others to take part. After some years, other priorities appear. There may be a building to extend, ministry to elderly people to consider, inter-denominational events to organise. New gifts are needed as new opportunities present themselves and the pastor, like the good servants in the parable of the talents, needs to multiply his or her gifts to cope. The new gifts operate in the same way as the old ones, and are obtained in the same way, but they are new. Perhaps, for instance, the minister begins to launch out into a healing ministry and has to start from first principles the way he or she did with children's work. Faith and prayer are called for, but it is one of the most wonderful things to watch when, in mid-life, a successful pastor is willing to take risks to add a new field of ministry to the one already cultivated.

Questions

1. Examine your own life. Does your character allow your gifts to be used to the full?
2. Are there gifts you need to take your ministry foward? Have you seriously prayed about this?
3. If you are a pastor, are you carrying out the full range of possible tasks implied by your ministry?
4. Are you in danger of burnout? Do you need help?

References

Francis, L.J. and Jones, S.H. (eds) (1996), *Psychological Perspectives on Christian Ministry*, Leominster: Gracewing.

"Dad, does responsibility hurt?"
"No, Son, it just takes time"

Chapter 6

THE MINISTER'S PERSONAL RESPONSIBILITIES

Bible Basis *Matthew 4:17*
Romans 13:7
Ephesians 5:22–6:9
1 Peter 3:7

The Child Support Agency in Britain was set up to force absentee fathers to take financial responsibility for their children. The agency has come in for considerable criticism and had to modify its working practices, but its founding premise is that adults should be responsible for their actions.

Alcoholics Anonymous treats men and women who want to overcome alcoholism. The first step towards recovery is the alcoholic's admission that there is a problem. Without this admission, the heavy drinking is 'normal', 'someone else's fault' or a 'temporary lapse'. Only by facing up to responsibility for one's actions is it possible to begin to find a remedy.

A Christian minister fell into depression and sin. He was allowed home by the social workers who had taken him into care. He began to receive help from other Christians. His story was that what had happened to him was 'all the devil's fault'. He was encouraged to begin ministering again and received prayer. Some time later he fell into depression and sin again. He had not taken responsibility for his actions. It was still 'all the devil's fault'.

Although Christians vary in their view of the relationship between free will and the will of God, the call of Christ to repent makes little

sense unless people are in control of their own behaviour (Mt 4:17).
Why should Jesus have called on men and women to repent, to turn
from sin, if obedience to such a call was beyond their power?

The effective Christian minister must be a person willing to take
responsibility or, to put this another way, be willing to be held accountable for a range of activities. There are four activity areas we draw
attention to here: business life, the home, spiritual life, personal charity
and evangelism.

Business life

The minister must be efficient in the conduct of ordinary business life.
Letters must be answered, phone calls returned, bills paid and minutes
read.

Letters and phone calls now, thanks to modern technology, can be
partly classified together in the sense that phone calls can be directed
onto an answer phone and dealt with at a convenient moment. Where
this is so, the minister must have a policy for dealing with what
can become a mountainous correspondence task. The rule that
every piece of paper should be only handled once is a good one.
Each letter is filed, answered or thrown away. By treating each piece
of paper in this way, it is possible to avoid a gathering collection of
litter on the minister's desk. Each stored phone call is treated like
paper.

The minister's filing system and diary work in tandem. The filing
system is likely to expand over the years and so it is worth giving
thought to its basic structure before ministerial life becomes too hectic.
Some people file everything under the name of the originator of a
document. Others file according to the subject the document covers.
Some have several filing systems related to each other through a
computerised database. Whichever system is adopted, it must be capable of expansion and each piece of paper must be placed where it can
be found again.

The minister's diary (or filofax) is a crucial book. Again, it may be
computerised and held on a laptop. More probably, it will be carried
around and a major panic follows if it is lost. Duplicates of important

information need therefore to be held, and it is helpful to keep diaries (or filofaxes) from previous years if anything needs to be checked on or if arrangements for an annual event need to be repeated. The most basic information held by diary will be in the form of appointments, preaching engagements, conference dates and the like. Most diaries include a yearly planning chart to allow the minister to see where the most crowded part of the year comes and, if he or she is wise, the minister will often put holiday dates into the system before anything else to avoid the position where the holiday is simply swept away by the demands of the work in hand. By the same token, the minister's day off in the week should be programmed in and kept sacrosanct.

The minister's diary must be correlated with the family calendar. All too often the minister's spouse finds that non-church-related appointments clash with a service, committee or conference. One system that works well is that a family calendar in the kitchen records the activities of all members of the household. There is a parents' evening on a particular date, a dental appointment on another, a visit from a relative on another and the

> one system that works well is that a family calendar in the kitchen records the activities of all members of the household

minister simply transfers his or her activities onto the family calendar so that everyone knows what everyone else is doing. If the minister is asked to do something, then he or she looks at the family calendar to ensure there is a gap before accepting the invitation. In this way the minister's family is not made to feel it is constantly placed second to the demands of other people.

The minister's family may need to be trained to take phone calls that come in live. They should record the name of the caller, the time of the call, the gist of the message and the return phone number. The disadvantage of an answer phone, of course, is that it inevitably puts the minister's phone bill up since incoming calls must be returned at the minister's expense. For this reason, it is beneficial to have a church policy about funding phone calls. The advantage of an answer phone, however, is that the phone can be safely ignored. As one minister said, 'when I am praying or eating, I am praying or eating, not answering the phone'.

Phones, if they are not connected to an answer phone, are a constant source of interruption. Methods of working vary and will depend on the kind of ministerial task being engaged on and the personality of the minister. Lloyd-Jones (1971) insisted that mornings must be absolutely safeguarded to allow the minister to pray and study. The phone would not be answered before lunch or, alternatively, it would be answered by someone other than the minister and the caller would be asked to ring back or an appointment made for the afternoon. By this means the minister has a measure of control over the pace of life. Yet some ministers may prefer to make phone calls themselves in the morning and do their studying later in the day or in the evening. The clash here, though, is that much ministerial work takes place in the evening. The determining factors, in the end, are the kind of pastoral ministry in view and the natural work cycle of the pastor. A prison chaplain will fit life into a different framework from a church pastor; some people may find they are at their most creative in the morning, others in the evening (Oswald, 1980). Quietness and reflection away from the phone are the objective and imperative if ministry is to remain fruitful.

Answering letters can be the bugbear of the minister's life. Solutions to this problem may be to learn to type, to become familiar with word-processing, to employ a secretary (perhaps someone in the congregation who will be paid by the church) or to develop expertise in the use of notelets and postcards for handwritten replies. The whole process can be speeded up by ordering stamps in large quantities which may be counted against legitimate expenses and buying postal scales so that letters can be costed and posted without time-consuming visits to the post office. But letters must be answered as matters of courtesy and integrity.

The use of fax and e-mail promises to become more common despite ministerial resistance to technological innovation. E-mail is particularly valuable since it can be read at the end of a day if necessary, comes straight to a convenient computer terminal and costs relatively little.

The payment of bills is of paramount importance. The minister who, because it is common practice in the world of commerce, routinely waits for the final demand from companies violates the injunction 'let no debt remain outstanding' (Rom 13:8). The man or woman who fails to pay bills out of apathy or dishonesty has no place in the ministry. This applies both to bills related to the church and to personal life. There is a case, of course, for waiting till a monthly stipend arrives before settling a bill, but in general nothing is gained by delaying payment. The only exception to this applies to cases where goods are held on approval and may be returned after a trial period. Clearly in this instance, ministers are not in breach of trust if they test the goods before paying. In the case of credit cards, there is normally a regular day in the month by which payment must be made to avoid incurring interest. To pay by this date is a matter of stewardship both because the interest charge is avoided and because credit cards often provide protection against faulty goods. To this extent credit cards are preferable to cash transactions.

The minister's personal finances fit into this category. These finances may well become complex if the minister is in receipt of allowances as part of stipend and in receipt of expenses for attendance at specific meetings. The possibility of confusing personal and professional finances is considerable and it is not uncommon to find ministers who are completely at sea in everything to do with figures and taxation. There are two solutions to this problem. The minister may either become expert in the subject by dint of reading the tax office

> the possibility of confusing personal and professional finances is considerable

brochures or may engage an accountant, which is normally a more expensive option. We would advise the minister to take the trouble to understand the tax system and to spend a day with a calculator and, if necessary, a financially competent friend to grasp the essentials of the subject.

Many ministers find themselves on committees. These can become an obsessional activity and completely erode any sense of calling or spirituality. It has been said that 'when God wants to move, he sets people praying and when the devil wants to stop God's people moving, he sets up a committee'. This an over cynical view, but the chairperson of a committee and the secretary have a responsibility to treat agenda items with integrity and not to allow committee procedures either to destroy personal relationships or to be completely distorted by personal relationships. In essence a committee, if it functions correctly, should allow collective wisdom and will to be brought to bear on a problem. Ministers, if they are placed on committees, ought to read the minutes of meetings, ensure that the minutes are accurate, scrutinise finances and attend punctually. If they are impatient with such details, they should not agree to serve on committees.

The minister's responsibilities in respect of his or her family (see below) include the financial dimension. There is a strong case for seeing *life insurance and pension contributions* as part of the minister's provision for his or her family. Ministers vary in their opinions on these matters. Some feel they cannot afford such contributions, others feel that they should 'take no thought for the morrow' and others that faith precludes payments for eventualities that providence might prevent. The view we take is that, at least in the area of pensions, ministers are foolish to make no pension contributions since these may simply be viewed as payments in advance to a period when earnings are reduced. It is not an indication of lack of faith to make pension contributions, rather it is an indication of lack of faith not to make

> it is not an indication of lack of faith to make pension contributions, rather it is an indication of lack of faith not to make them

them. In the case of life insurance, we have seen the widows of ministers under immense financial pressure because no provision was made. The premiums simply buy income in the event of death, and nobody knows how long their life will be. There are promises of long life in the Scripture to those who honour their parents (Eph 6:2), but there are also scriptural examples of godly people, like Stephen and John the Baptist, whose lives were cut short.

The home

The minister's responsibilities in the home include all those things that make a good father or a good mother. The primary relationship in the minister's life, after that with God, is with the spouse. This relationship must be maintained in good repair. The New Testament shows husband and wife praying together (1 Pet 3:7), enjoying sexual relations (1 Cor 7:5), loving and respecting one another (Eph 5:22,25) and bringing up children jointly (Eph 6:1). The Old Testament shows marriage as being designed to produce 'godly offspring' (Mal 3:15), and there is empirical evidence showing that many ministers grew up in homes where both parents are church attenders. 'How do you ensure your children continue in the church?' asked a young minister to a successful older one whose two sons were in the ministry. 'I made Christianity fun when they were young' the old man replied. So the ministerial parent should have no qualms about doing the sorts of things with children that they enjoy, whether it be going to a concert or taking them camping.

Although it is impossible to lay down rules for a Christian home that will fit every situation and occasion, we take the view that it is important for the Christian family to eat together at least once a day. Grace before meals ensures that there is an opportunity to pray together (however briefly) and has the practical purpose of ensuring that everyone starts the meal simultaneously. But eating together implies that the television does not dominate the life of the household and that every member of the family can talk with any other. Also important, especially when children are young, is to pray with them, and this is a responsibility that rests with both parents, not with the mother only.

A policy of discipline in the home is essential to a happy atmosphere. Mothers and fathers may have different priorities in children's behaviour and they need to talk about these differences out of the children's earshot. The basic idea of discipline is that a graduated series of rewards or punishments may be used to encourage behaviour that is desired and discourage behaviour that is detested. This may sound a mechanical scheme and it can only avoid falling into this trap if parents enjoy and appreciate their children – in other words, if the reward for the children is to spend time with parents in conversation or a game. Quite simple rewards (a sweet, a hug) can have an enormous affect on children's behaviour, and quite simple punishments ('I am disappointed in you Tommy') can be salutary. Large rewards or punishments are appropriate to the action; if the parent only uses the extremes of reward or punishment, there is no sanction left for extreme behaviour.

There are two mistakes that parents must at all costs avoid. The first is to use rewards and punishments erratically. Sometimes the child can stay up late, at other times the child is sent to bed early, and there is no rhyme or reason that the child can grasp for the sudden switches in parental policy or mood. Erratic parental behaviour will produce erratic child behaviour. This leads to the second mistake to avoid. The parent must explain why particular actions are being taken ('You must not ride your bike tomorrow because today

> erratic parental behaviour will produce erratic child behaviour

you rode it dangerously'). If the parent uses rewards and punishments without explanation, the child will become an outward conformist with no inward acceptance of the values the parent is trying to instill. It is the explanations to the child that build the values on which the parent is basing his or her behaviour. Eventually, when the child grows up, it will continue to keep to the values the parent has taught because it wishes to and not because it must do.

The wider family responsibilities extend to relatives and in-laws. Practical help, prayer, hospitality and love should be part of the minister's lifestyle. Elderly parents may require accommodation or visits and the minister may be in a position to co-ordinate the necessary support.

Spiritual life

Jesus, quoting the book of Deuteronomy, said 'Worship the Lord your God, and serve him only' (Mt 4:10). The order is important. Worship comes first, service second. Without worship service can become a burden and an extra duty to be thanklessly performed. When worship is enjoyed, the whole scene is transformed. Worship of God enables the minister to maintain a larger vision and a proper motivation. Service is undertaken with enthusiasm and spiritual sensitivity.

The spiritual life of the minister is best safeguarded by a regular time of personal prayer each day. There is no need to become bound by a set of rules (the prayer time must be first thing in the morning or last thing at night), but it must be a conscious part of the minister's day. The advantage of an early prayer time is that the day is quiet and lies ahead. The minister can consider the events in prospect and pray about them, ask for strength or guidance, and begin to have a sense for God's will in what lies ahead. Certainly Jesus prayed early in the morning (Mk 1:35) and, when reached by his disciples, said, 'Let us go somewhere else – to the nearby villages – so that I can preach there also'. His prayer was associated with the preaching life, and the same pattern can be seen in the way the apostles of the early church organised their time. After appointing others to deal with the demanding practical task of arranging for the charitable distribution of food, Peter said, 'We will give our attention to prayer and the ministry of the word' (Acts 6:4). On the other hand, Jesus also prayed at night, and did so before selecting the twelve apostles (Lk 6:12,13).

> the advantage of an early prayer time is that the day is quiet and lies ahead

Along with the minister's spiritual life is the mental life. There is a strong case for periods of study as a means of finding a path out of an impasse. Study opens the minister to fresh ideas and enables the re-examination of presuppositions and theories. There is a whole series of mid-ministry courses open to the minister and these offer helpful perspectives and intellectual recharging.

Personal charity and evangelism

By virtue of the minister's position, he or she is likely to receive mailshots asking for charitable donations, sometimes at the rate of one a day. There is a dilemma to resolve here. Should the minister support a large number of organisations with a small amount each, or should he or she select one or two and support them as much as possible? In either case, it is sensible to keep a rough tally of the amount given each year. Moreover, this tally may be effectively increased by using the tax system's inducements to charitable giving. In Britain deeds of covenant or gift allow the recipient to claim back the tax that was paid on the money given.

Opportunities for personal evangelism will also be presented and the minister should not be shy of taking them. In many instances people expect the minister to advocate a spiritual answer to solutions and may be disappointed if nothing is said.

If the minister refrains from personal charity or personal evangelism, his or her ministry is likely to become slightly hollow. Encouragement to the congregation to be charitable or evangelistic will become unrealistic in the light of the minister's failure along these lines.

Questions

1. List the areas in your life on which you take responsibility (are held accountable) by other human beings.
2. Do you find it easy to take responsibility, or would you rather someone else took it? Use this question to reflect on your pattern of life.
3. Can you take responsibility for business matters without taking responsibility for spiritual matters, or do you see the two as being related? Try to disentangle these two parts of your life.
4. In the light of what you have read in this chapter, which responsibilities do you need to take more seriously? What are you going to do about it?

References

Lloyd-Jones, M. (1971), *Preachers and Preaching*, London: Hodder and Stoughton.

Oswald, I. (1980), *Sleep* (4th edition), Harmondsworth: Penguin.

"Well, Pastor, you've certainly got the church moving"

Chapter 7

THE MINISTER'S CONGREGATION

Bible Basis   *Acts 2:17*
                     Acts 10 and 11

For most ministers pastoral care takes place in the context of attachment to a congregation. This chapter deals with the leadership, management and discipline of a congregation, but much of what is said could be adapted to other settings. We begin with the vision of the minister for the work to which he or she is called.

Vision

The often quoted text 'Where there is no vision, the people perish' (Prov 29:18, AV) has been used by ministers to justify the inauguration of change in the life of the congregation. Without a vision, it is argued, people perish. There must, therefore, be a vision of some kind. The vision may be for a new building, a new evangelistic programme or social initiative, and it almost does not matter what the vision is about as long as it is there. In effect the vision is a holy 'idea' or 'plan' sometimes treated as if it is not susceptible to examination or challenge.

In his sermon on the Day of Pentecost, Peter quotes from the Book of Joel and characterises the pentecostal nature of the church. 'Your young men will see visions, and your old men will dream dreams' (Acts 2:18). The justification for the notion of vision comes in this verse. And, yes, ministers and others should see visions and dream dreams; they should be people of daring revelation and inspired by the Holy Spirit to see a better future. But, if the text of Acts is examined to find out how Peter's pentecostal announcement worked out in practice, there are four visions recorded. All are important, though not in quite the way the word is often used today.

The first concerns the conversion of Paul and his reception into the church at Damascus. Ananias sees a vision of Christ and is told to go to pray with the blinded Paul (Acts 9:10–19). The vision serves to give Ananias confidence to meet the prime persecutor of the church and it must have been important to Paul as a way of confirming the reality of his own experience. It is a vision that launches Paul out into a preaching ministry.

The second concerns Peter in Joppa (Acts 10, 11). Here Peter is praying at around midday when he sees a sheet full of animals let down from heaven and hears a voice telling him to kill and eat. Three times he is told to eat, and three times he refuses. Immediately afterwards, three men arrive asking him to visit the home of a Roman centurion who is a convert, or partial convert, to Judaism. The next day Peter goes to the Roman household and preaches the Gospel to the assembled crowd. The Holy Spirit falls, there is speaking in tongues and Peter baptises the new converts to Christianity in water. It is clear that the vision to eat the unclean animals was a sign to Peter that the church was henceforward no longer to be an exclusively Jewish community, but was to be open to a Gentile mission. The vision marked a new stage in the life of the church, a new ministry and a new set of problems. Only Peter, with a Jewish-only mentality, could convincingly break this news to the Jerusalem church, and only a vision could confirm to Peter that the new direction was given by God.[2]

The third vision concerns Paul on the second missionary journey. The Gospel has so far been preached in Asia minor, but no step has been taken by the apostles to cross to the European mainland, to Greece and the regions beyond. Paul tries to evangelise in Mysia and Bithynia and fails. 'The Spirit of Jesus' would not allow it (Acts 16:7) and so he comes to Troy where he receives a vision of a man from Macedonia who begs him to come over and help. This vision sets Paul free to cross the sea to Neapolis and from there to Philippi where he founds a church and is imprisoned for his pains. The vision served to give Paul clear direction, a fresh territory to preach in and work that kept him occupied for part of the most fruitful period of his life.

[2.] Cornelius the Centurion receives a vision earlier in the chapter, but this does not invalidate the general point we are making. Visions are about new directions and turning points.

The fourth vision concerns Paul while he is in Corinth (Acts 18:9). The indications are that Paul will be imprisoned or arrested again (as he has been at Philippi) and he is presumably tempted to leave before trouble flares up. In a vision Christ tells Paul to remain where he is. A while later Paul is dragged before the civic authorities, but a legal judgement is given in his favour, a judgement that has beneficial repercussions for the early church for several years.

When the early church saw visions, then, these were crucial moments, and not simply moments related to the growth and progress of individual congregations. None of the visions recorded here is relevant to the buying of buildings or the leadership structure of a congregation.

But does this mean that ministers should have no plans for the future, no ideas about possible lines of action? God forbid! Ministers undoubtedly need to have plans, but we contend that these arise from general biblical principles. The minister needs to be able to look at the empty church building or the tough council estate and see what might be done by faith. As a leader of a congregation the minister can then communicate realistic hopes to the flock without having to overclaim by pretending that his 'vision' comes hot from heaven and must be fulfilled in every detail. On the contrary plans based on general biblical principles may change and adapt to circumstances and what is important is the result of those plans in the long run.

Leadership

Style and structure

Within the church a variety of leadership styles is in place. There are *democratic* styles where each decision is discussed and voted upon or a consensus sought, sometimes at church meetings and at others in committees. There are *autocratic* styles where one or two individuals insist that they have God-given authority to make decisions that nobody must gainsay, and there are *theocratic* styles where the leader is God, though often working through established and recognised procedures. There may also be a mixture of styles such that an autocrat claims to be acting theocratically, or where a democratic style is used for consultation but not for decision-making.

These styles, much discussed and important though they are, must be seen within two wider contexts. The first is the general history of the church throughout the ages. Autocrats do well, but after they die their legacy is often disappointing since their followers cannot replace them and dissension breaks out. Democrats also do well, but infrequently make radical decisions. Theocracy is rarely practised effectively and, in the biblical period of the Judges when it was the norm, charismatic leaders emerged to meet the challenge of specific national dangers. The uncertainty of theocratic leadership led the people of Israel to ask for a king, a request reluctantly granted, and only partly successful.

The second context is that of the New Testament. Although there is clear and definite leadership within the early church, the structure of this leadership varied from congregation to congregation. For example, the Philippian congregation had elders and deacons, but the Corinthian congregation has no mention of these offices (Dunn, 1990). It has been argued that the New Testament gives us general principles to be flexibly applied: there must be leadership, often collective, with a wide range of tasks and specialisms. But there is no fixed pattern applied universally.

We argue that there is certainly an optimum leadership structure (applied below) because the dangers of dictatorship must be counterbalanced by the dangers of leaderlessness. Unaccountable dictators in the church are a menace, but equally a jumble of ungovernable congregational members is a danger to the spiritual life of those involved. Biblical leadership shuns both these extremes.

Charity law relating to churches in Britain is extremely complicated and has long historical roots. There are specific statutes to which the larger denominations must refer and which were enacted by Parliament specifically with their needs in mind. It should be stressed that ministers ought to consult their denomination's legal experts to ensure they are correctly advised. In addition, the Charity Commissioners issue helpful leaflets dealing with charity law.[3] We give examples drawn from British Assemblies of God since this is the group we know best, but some of these provisions are unlikely to apply in other denominational groups. For example, many denominations have a Board of Trustees responsible for the management of property and local trustees must consult this Board.

Normally, especially where property or finances are concerned, it is the trust deed which is particularly important. The concept of a charitable trust is, in essence, quite simple: it is that property purchased

[3.] CC3 Deals with *Responsibility of Charity Trustees*, CC11 with *Renumeration of Charity trustees* and CC28 with *Charity Land*. Further information can be obtained from The Charity Commissioners, St Albans House, 57-60 Haymarket, London SW1Y 4QX.

or money owned by a group of people should be held by a much smaller group (usually the trustees) and used only for specific purposes. These specific purposes are laid down when the trust is first formed.

Since the trustees (as they are usually called) control the finance or property on behalf of others, they should not themselves benefit financially from their position.

In the case of evangelical churches the deed lays down the *objects of the trust* (usually to advance the Christian religion and the furtherance of the Gospel by the preaching and teaching of the Word of God; to pursue charitable purposes related to the first aim) and in some cases *membership conditions* of the church.

Within Assemblies of God in Great Britain and Ireland the management of the church is vested in the Church Council which comprises the minister and duly appointed or elected leaders. The Church Council is responsible for keeping a list of the names of church members. The names and addresses of members of the Church Council must be kept in church records. The Council must have a chairperson, secretary and treasurer, and the chairperson should be the senior minister of the church, unless a decision is made otherwise.

It should be noted, however, that the kinds of trust deeds accepted by the Charity Commissioners (the body looking after charity law in England and Wales) for local assemblies within Assemblies of God are exceptional in several respects.

These respects are:

1. In Assemblies of God the Church Council may contain members of the church who are paid by the church *so long as they are in a minority on the Council.* Normally salaried members cannot sit on the decision-making body of the charity.
2. In Assemblies of God the Minister may be a member of the trustees, even though he is paid by the church. Normally trustees cannot be remunerated (apart from receiving incidental expenses).
3. In Assemblies of God the Church Council is the decision-making body in the local church as far as the Charity Commissioners are concerned. Normally the trustees are the decision-making body. In the model trust deed used in local Assemblies of God assemblies the holding trustees are directed by the Church Council and must carry out any lawful direction.

The Church Council must meet at least four times a year and regulate its own proceedings and make regulations to deal with the appointment of ministers, elders, deacons and other appointees. Everyone paid by the church is under contract to the Church Council. In addition there must be an annual general meeting at which reports by the officers of the church and the published accounts of the previous financial year must be given.

In Assemblies of God it is the holding trustees who hold the land and buildings of the church, and these are appointed by the Church Council, though not necessarily members of it. These holding trustees must act in accordance with the lawful directions of the Church Council.

The legal structure ensures three basic things:

• that the church exists for charitable objects;
• that the basis of paid employment by the church is contractually specified;
• that annual reports and accounts are given to recognised church members.

This legal structure is not drawn from the New Testament so that the biblical concepts of call, ministerial gifting, pastors, elders and deacons are absent. It is, however, compatible with the New Testament order.

The New Testament describes elders (1 Tim 3:1–7; see also chapter 4), deacons (1 Tim 3:12–13), apostles, prophets, evangelists, pastors and teachers (Eph 4:1–14). The terms 'bishop', 'overseer' and 'pastor' are used interchangeably in Acts 20.[4] Broadly speaking, the meaning of the terms is straightforward enough: elders, bishops, overseers and pastors are involved in caring for people and may be involved in teaching within the church. Deacons appear to have a practical function, though the issue can be confused because 'deacon' in Greek means a 'servant', and the apostles describe themselves as being 'servants of the word of God' (Acts 6:4). In this sense all the Christian roles listed above are truly servants. But it does seem, from Acts 6, that there were recognised people chosen to perform a high-profile practical task – to arrange for the distribution of food – and that this role was later formalised within ordinary congregations in the office of deacon. In short, there is a contrast between overseers who must be able to teach and deacons who do not have to (1 Tim 3).

[4.] The *elders* are told that the holy spirit has made them *overseers* and so they should *shepherd* (=*pastor*) the flock (v.28). The overseers of Acts 20:28 is the *bishop* of 1 Timothy 3:1.

Throughout this book we have tried to use the word 'minister' as the best translation to cover every kind of Christian servanthood.

When all this is applied within the life of a modern congregation, we may end up with a group of elders, or a single pastor or clergy person, a board of deacons and other appointments with ministerial functions (perhaps an evangelist, worship leader, housegroup leader or Sunday school superintendent). We would argue that, whatever the

> there is a contrast between overseers who must be able to teach and deacons who do not have to

structure, the pastoral functions should be in general control and not be controlled by the diaconate. The pastoral ministry, fired by love and evangelism, should move the life of the church forward. If the diaconate takes control, the pastoral functions are treated purely as if they amount to secular employment and decisions are dictated by the availability of money, of which there is always a shortage.

The optimum structure for congregational leadership, and the one we believe comes closest to a biblical norm, sees a pastor whose evident calling and gifting place him or her at the helm, supported by a group of functioning elders (not simply peo-

> the pastoral functions should be in general control and not be controlled by the diaconate

ple chosen to make up the numbers or because they are socially desirable) to which a body of deacons is responsible. This body of deacons may themselves be in charge of free-standing sections of the church's life (for instance its ministry in music), and each deacon may have a department to look after.

The following table shows how easily the requirements of British charity law and a biblical pattern can be allied using the trust deed Assemblies of God have agreed with the Charity Commissioners:

Membership of the Church Council can, in other words, be determined by a pastor or elders. Or, to put this another way, the pastoral team, could, if it wished, become the Church Council. In practice it is wise to ensure representation from non-pastoral sections of the church, particularly since a formal annual report must be made to church members. Charity law rightly insists that church members should know how the money they give is being spent.

Legal structure	Biblical pattern A	Biblical pattern B
Minister	Minister supported by elders and deacons. Minister meets elders separately from deacons.	Senior ministers and other ministers supported by deacons
Church Council	Minister with elders, deacons and some holding trustees. Treasurer and secretary serve this group, but are not necessarily members of it.	Senior minister and other ministers;one to serve as treasurer and another as secretary, alternatively a treasurer and secretary are chosen to serve this group, but are not necessarily members of it.
Holding trustees	Minister is permitted to be a member of the holding trustees	Minister is permitted to be a member of the holding trustees
Church members	Church members	Church members

Decision-making:

Most churches have separate groups for separate types of decision. Ministers make decisions about spiritual matters, and deacons make decisions about material matters.

This sounds an easy distinction, but it can become confused. If spiritual decisions cost money, then deacons may wish to be consulted or to object. The possibility of conflict is real and most ministers would agree that, if the diaconate overrules the pastoral oversight, the tail is wagging the dog. Yet, if the pastoral oversight is financially irresponsible, someone needs to say so.

> ministers make decisions about spiritual matters, and deacons make decisions about material matters

Happy congregations are those where decisions are made by the appropriate group and then explained to the other groups. In this way, the pastoral oversight can make a decision, explain it to the diaconate and then together, acting as the Church Council, explain it to the whole church. An annual general meeting of church members can then endorse what church leaders have already decided.

There are purely material matters (should the Gents toilet be re-painted? Who is going to cut the grass? Does the minibus need new tyres?) that ought to be entirely in the hands of the diaconate. The Pastoral Oversight should not be bothered with these matters, and the prospect of a meeting of the whole church to discuss this is ridiculous. The entire purpose of a diaconate is to handle these matters on behalf of the church.

There are also matters that concern the trustees that do not need to concern other groups within the church, though experience suggests that trustees, after a building has been bought or extended, tend to have only a small amount to do. Perhaps there is a dispute about car parking or maybe a playgroup wants to hire the church hall? These are matters that strictly speaking concern the trustees, but may be dis-cussed by the deacons, especially if one or more of the trustees also serve on the diaconate.

Management: general

We believe that management is concerned with planning, organisation, communication and motivation. Together these activities complement the basics of leadership.

Planning

This belongs to each decision-making group in the church. There may be planning by the pastoral oversight, by the deacons, the Church Council or the trustees. Any group can project its activities into the future and try to arrange them in a sensible sequence.

The usual division into short-term and long-term planning is help-ful. Short-term planning applies to convenient chunks of time. A group meeting every month might call planning for the next three months short-term planning. A group meeting every six months might call short-term planning anything that applied to the coming year. Short-term planning operates with fairly predictable and controllable events.

Short-term planning ought to be fairly accurate. We know the date of Christmas or when the summer holidays start. We can fix the date of a carol service or work out when children's holiday clubs will be and make plans that prevent anything clashing.

Short-term planning sets objectives that are within range. Imagine two congregations. Congregation A wants to make 100 converts this year. Church B wishes to present the Gospel to every child in the housing estates to the west of the town and will do so by training teams to visit schools, individuals to visit homes and by holding children's clubs during the holidays. Church A is really wishing, Church B is operating a management plan.

Objectives are aims that have been translated into specific and achievable tasks. As they are fulfilled, we become more confident, and the people who are being led become more confident, that it will be possible to reach the next set of objectives. Reaching objectives is good for faith and good for leadership.

Long-term planning is strategic and has to be more vague. We have a general idea of what we would like the church to be like in five years, but there are too many uncertainties over such a period of time to allow us to be sure of what will happen. One minister feels that the church should become more involved with missions and another that the church should relate more directly to the local community. Experience suggests that the fulfilment of long-term plans is often dependent on factors beyond our control. All we can do is to be ready for circumstances to favour and fit our aspirations, and this keeps us praying. Long-term plans will influence and shape our next set of short-term plans.

But how do we plan? In a Christian context plans begin with prayer and concern. Paul speaks of his planned visits to the church in Corinth (2 Cor 1:17). The plans had been laid with great seriousness: 'when I planned this, did I do it lightly?' No. On this occasion, however, the plans were changed 'to spare' the church a painful visit, when apostolic discipline would have been enforced (v. 23). The change was made out of care for the Corinthians and not out of fickleness.

The original plan, then, was intended to make the best possible use of Paul's time since the churches in Macedonia would have one visit and the more troublesome church in Corinth would have two visits within the same basic journey.

Paul's long-term planning is illustrated by the writing of the Letter to the Romans. This letter, sent to prepare the church for Paul's proposed visit to Rome (Rom 1:10–15), was composed before the money collected from the Greek churches had been taken to Jerusalem (Rom 15:26), and the mention of Phoebe and Gaius (Rom 16:1,23) suggest the letter was written from Corinth or not far away. The likely date was AD 57, but Paul did not get to Rome for at least another two years. In other words, while he was in Greece and before he returned east to Jerusalem, his mind was already turning west to Rome and a possible mission in Spain (Rom 15:22–29).

Whether long or short-term, planning has to take people into account. Paul shows this. He writes to the Corinthians and to the Romans. In the local church, too, planning is people-based, people-specific. It is alert to the personal situations. Paul knows that his plans will have to mesh in with the plans of other people. But the actual practicalities of planning demand organisation.

Organisation

This starts with the minister him or herself. We have already spoken of the minister's personal responsibilities, and these imply an organised lifestyle. Organisation goes beyond the home into the church. The minister is a person whose use of time and resources are properly deployed. 'Teach us to number our days aright, that we may gain a heart of wisdom' was the prayer of Moses (Ps 90:12).

The minister needs a framework for the day and for the week. The framework will change if the minister is travelling abroad or preaching every night in an evangelistic campaign. It will adjust to the times and seasons of church life. A framework, once adopted however, prevents hours of agonising decision-making. It builds in time for rest and travel. For example, perhaps, as we suggest in chapter 4, prayer and study take place in the morning, visiting and appointments in the afternoon and preaching and teaching in the evening.

Within the framework the minister needs a diary and a year planner. Engagements can then be marked in, prepared for and fulfilled on time. High priority events can be given extra time in preparation. The minister's working life is divided between public activities (leading services, taking part in committees and conferences), private activities (like prayer, meditation and study) and semi-private activities (like counselling or personal evangelism). The framework allows a balance between these activities.

Within the church, organisation is essential to its success. Play is often made on the distinction between an organism and an organisation. The church is a body (Rom 12), and therefore an organism, where every part is related to every other in a living way. An organisation is more abstract, more systems-orientated or task-orientated, and not necessarily alive. Yet, the distinction is easy to exaggerate. The church is organised, and that is something common to both an organism and an organisation. 'For God is not a God of disorder but of peace' (1 Cor 14:33).

Church organisation occurs when a job is identified and an individual is related to that job so that it may be carried out effectively. Mr Smith is asked to greet people at the church door one Sunday morning and Mrs Smith is asked to take a crèche on the same morning. The Smith family ar-

> the church is organised, an
> that is something common
> both an organism and an
> organisation

rives early at church that morning because Mr and Mrs Smith both have a job to do. But Mrs Smith is a nurse who works a night shift every third week so this week must be avoided for both her and her husband. Organisation ensures that this willing couple is able to be in the right place at the right time without clashing with their other commitments.

The process of organisation must identify the person or group who make decisions. Who is in charge of the Sunday school? Who organises the rota for greeting arrivals at the church door? In most churches the minister will not want to be locked into the small print of the rotas, but he or she may well want to ensure that the right person looks after the Sunday school and be involved or consulted about any decisions made in the Sunday school that have a knock-on effect into the life of the congregation as a whole. If the minister is the chief organiser, as is usually the case, then he or she is responsible for ensuring that everyone affected understands where decisions for a particular activity are being made. The process of organisation, in effect, depends on the ability to delegate.

When should *delegation* take place? We suggest six signs the minister should look out for:

- when it becomes necessary to organise;
- when the minister has people who need new worlds to conquer;
- when the minister is doing trivial tasks others could be trained to do;
- when the minister is overworked;
- when the minister is missing deadlines;
- when the minister is aware of frequent crises within the church.

How should delegation take place? We suggest delegation has three components:

1. the assignment of a task;
2. an assignment of authority to carry out the task;
3. a person to whom the delegate is accountable.

The task, or area of responsibility, should be clearly outlined to avoid confusion. 'Here are the objectives, and these are the means to achieve them.' The delegate should understand that authority for the task goes with accountability. 'Here is the key to the minor hall, and here is the money you will need to buy the equipment.' The delegate should report back to the minister, or whoever is appropriate, especially at the beginning, to ensure that all is going well. 'Come to see me next month to chat over how it is working out.'

What tends to happen is that the minister will see a promising member of the congregation and talk privately to him or her. 'Think about this task in the church. Pray about it. I believe you will be able to do it well', the minister says. After a while, the member of the congregation returns with a decision and then, if the decision is favourable, a public announcement is made. 'Starting from next month Mrs Smith will be in charge of the crèche. She will draw up the rota. Please take your problems to her!'

Delegation leads to *departments within the church*. And these departments relate to the basic structure of minister, elders, deacons, Church Council, and so on, mentioned earlier. Here is one structure that works well:

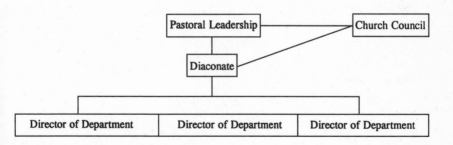

Each department will often have a style of its own: those engaged on prison visiting may be young, single and interested in Christian rock music; those teaching in the Sunday school may be young married couples who are juggling career and family commitments; those engaged in youth work may be an older married couple with teenage children. People will often work in more than one department. But the point is that each department should know what it wishes to achieve and how to communicate with the rest of the church. It should have its own sense of being a team without becoming a clique.

The more formal sections of the church will take minutes of their meetings and work to an agenda. Trustees' and deacons' meetings are likely to fall into this category, and the annual general meeting should certainly be put on this basis.

There are Christians who dislike being tied down to agendas and minutes and feel such an apparatus is unspiritual - and so it can be. Yet, it needn't be. After all, an agenda simply sets out a list of the things that are to be discussed and done and the order in which they will be tackled, and minutes simply record what was decided on the last occasion everyone met.

An agenda will ensure that the minutes of the previous meeting have been read and are agreed as a correct record: the importance of this is that disagreements about who was present or what was decided are cut out by this procedure. The minutes should not record every long and convoluted argument but only decisions that have been agreed and, very often, who has to carry out a particular task as a result of a group decision. It is the job of the secretary of a group to draw up the agenda, usually in consultation with others in the group, and, if possible, to circulate it in advance, stating when the meeting will begin, where it will take place and when it is expected to end.

Agenda
Meeting of .....
Date....   Starting.....   Finishing.....
1. Present were....
2. Minutes of the previous meeting to be agreed
3. Matters arising from the minutes
etc

The chairperson of the meeting has the task of ensuring that:
• the items on the agenda are adequately discussed;
• everyone present is able to make a contribution (i.e. not letting one person do all the talking);
• decisions are clearly made (by voting or by consensus);
• the meeting keeps to time.

Communication between departments

Communications between church departments and the rest of the congregation is a necessity. Rothauge (1985; quoted by Kaldor *et al.,* 1994) argues that there are four kinds of church, dependent on size:

Family Church (with fewer than 50 people): characterised by intimacy, where everyone knows everyone else.

Pastoral Church (50 to 150 people): increased size leads to a need for a cellular structure. It requires a centralised authority, usually the pastor, to co-ordinate activities.

Programme Church (150 to 350 people): this size marks a change from a highly relational to an organisational mode as the main mechanism for holding the congregation together. Attenders no longer find themselves automatically close to each other; this must be planned for through structured opportunities to associate with other members.

Corporation Church (over 350 people): the congregation is so large, and there are so many programmes and separate groups, that, to avoid fragmentation, there need to be regular church-wide celebrations, outreaches, and so on.

In congregations up to 150 people, it is enough to have a notice-board, notices on a Sunday morning and perhaps a weekly newsheet. A message given to the whole church will be picked up by those to whom it is relevant. 'There is a singing practice on Thursday night' does not apply to most people, but it is good that most people should have an idea of what is going on.

The problem for a Programme Church (over 150) is that it will often require more than one Sunday morning service and, when this happens, groups within the church which need to get in touch may well miss each other if they attend different services. It is still possible to use a newsheet and have Sunday morning notices, but these need to be planned at a longer distance in advance than is the case with smaller churches since it is not possible to make sudden changes on Sunday morning itself.

Statistics suggest that the average congregation in the western world has about 80 people. It is therefore a Pastoral Church and striving to become a Programme Church.[5] Contrary to expectation larger

[5.] Personal communication and calculation through Lausanne e-mail network. See also Chapter 1.

churches are not necessarily less friendly than smaller ones (Kaldor *et al.*, 1994: 134). The friendliness of the church is developed consciously by the pastoral ministry but also by following the policy that 'everyone needs to belong to a big group and a small group'. The big group gives identity and confidence; the small group gives individualised support and care.

The small group is sometimes called a 'cell' since this is the building block of life, and each cell is substantially self-sufficient. The cell may be a home group or a prayer unit and will encourage members to care for each other. Each cell may have a leader who carries out basic pastoral functions (enquiring about people's health if they are absent from church, praying for them, advising them) without being expected to give systematic teaching. 'Contrary to the stereotype of churchgoing as an impersonal duty performed on Sunday, churchgoing for most attenders involves being part of a network of caring relationships. These caring relationships are what they value most' (Kaldor *et al.,* 1994:193). The minister may think people come to church for his or her preaching, but often this is not so: it is the caring relationships that follow the preaching that many people appreciate, and the cell group simply offers another context where care may be expressed.

> everyone needs to belong to a big group and a small group

Young people are especially inclined to attend church for social reasons and pastoral care of teenagers needs to take this preference seriously. In an analysis of young British Baptists, it became clear that the young people who were beginning to slide away from the church did so for four reasons: they thought their Sunday morning services were boring, the sermons were unhelpful, their minister was out of date and that he failed to give them an opportunity to make decisions. They agreed that their minister was friendly. The problem was not over a personality clash with the minister but with the kind of message the minister preached and the kind of worship the main service offered: it did not reach the worries, lifestyle, temptations and concerns of young people (Kay and Francis, 1996). Of course young people can be selfish and hypercritical, and to pander to their wishes, may lead to the alienation of the older generation. But one thing both old and young can detect is whether there is life in the services.

Motivation

Motivation is what makes people want to be active. The minister has this responsibility. Little is more demoralising that to try to drag enthusiasm out of reluctant and semi-committed Christians. The minister, by preaching and example, must fire up the congregation without turning the sermon into a harangue for laziness. Good preaching imperceptibly chips away at our objections and excuses. Benjamin Franklin once listened to George Whitefield preach. Franklin, no believer himself, had decided to calculate the number of people who could hear Whitefield's oratory in the open air. He paced out

> **good preaching imperceptibly chips away at our objections and excuses**

the dimensions of the area where the crowd was silently standing. As he walked Franklin heard Whitefield make an appeal for money for an orphanage. Franklin records that, as he listened, he decided he would put the silver in his pocket in the collection. But, while the preaching continued and Franklin continued his pacing, he changed his mind, and decided to put the gold in his pocket when the collection bag came round. By the end of the sermon, however, he had changed his mind again and decided to put both the gold and the silver to help the poor children of the American east coast. Preaching is an appeal to the mind as well as to the heart.

Management: of change

The effect of the pastor's ministry will be seen in the congregation. Kaldor *et al.* (1994) have provided invaluable data on how groups within the church adapt to change. In Australia, a culture of choice prevails. A supermarket mentality ensures that young people are prepared to move church until they find what they want. An individualistic mentality ensures that young people live out their faith rather than to express it through mystery and ritual. This leads to the appearance of 'switchers', people who switch denominations, sometimes because they become unhappy with a church's prevalent theology and at other times because they feel their needs have changed. Conflict with congregational leaders appears in nearly a fifth of these cases. Switchers are younger, on average, than 'transfers', people who change congregations within the same denomination.

When the statistics showing the age profile of congregations against congregational size are examined, it is clear that the largest congregations in Australia (over 500 people) are also those with the greatest percentage of young people (in the 20–29 age bracket), while the smallest churches (under 50) have the highest percentage of older people (over 60 years of age). Since the switchers fit into the younger category normally, this suggests that the larger churches are also those which have gained by attracting Christians from other congregations. Analysis shows this to be the case. Large churches, which are attractive to newcomers (first time arrivals) are also those attractive to switchers.

> the largest congregations in Australia (over 500 people) are also those with the greatest percentage of young people

What is it that they find attractive? The most frequently cited reason for joining a congregation given by switchers and newcomers is personal contact. 'Friendship is the path for bringing people into the life of the church' (Kaldor *et al.*, 1994:160), and this is so with 47% of newcomers and 39% of switchers. Contact with clergy or a church activity account for a further 17% of newcomers and 10% of switchers. Transfers, as we might expect, go to a church because it is close by.

> friendship is the path for bringing people into the life of the church

What puts people off? In Kaldor's survey (which covered a great range of denominations), some 26% of 15–19 year olds have trouble with the language used in church, and 22% specifically have trouble in understanding the preaching. This implies that technical terms, Christian jargon and in-phrases obscure communication. How many people still ask for a 'word of prayer' (why only one?) or pray that the 'Lord will undertake' (is someone dead?) or think that the Lord's Supper should be at the end of the day?

There are very real differences between big and small congregations because the larger congregations offer a variety of services and activities and members tend to choose the ones they want. In a small church everyone is expected at every meeting. In a large church, attendance is selective. The management of change in different sizes of congregation will vary. In a large church, the need will be to diversify – to launch a new programme; in a small church, the need will be to make preparations for growth involving everyone.

The rate at which people accept change is partly linked to age. Younger people are generally quickest in accepting change and older people slowest, but there are exceptions and it would be wrong to dub every old person a 'stick in the mud'. About a quarter of those over 70 years of age are open to new initiatives, though the highest percentage of those who are open

> the figures also show that more highly educated members of the congregation are most open to change

to change (42%) is in the 30 to 49 age group. The figures also show that more highly educated members of the congregation are most open to change: 47% of those with a university degree, as compared with 31% of those who left school as soon as they could, are open to change (Kaldor *et al.*, 1994:22). Presumably education gives people a greater flexibility of thought and so a greater ability to cope with change.

Discipline

The sad duty of discipline certainly falls within the ambit of pastoral ministry. The instruction in Galatians 6 is explicit. 'If someone is caught in a sin, you who are spiritual should restore him gently. But watch yourself or you may be tempted.' Those who fall in to sin are to be restored and the Greek word here is used elsewhere for mending bones or repairing nets. The purpose of church discipline is to bring Christians back to usefulness and not to cast them into outer darkness.

Where someone falls into sin, the matter must be dealt with rapidly and fairly. It should be investigated (2 Cor 13:1; 1 Tim 5:19), judged (1 Cor 5:12) and, if necessary, a public announcement made to prevent speculation and gossip. The main reason for making a public announcement is that, in some instances, whatever has happened will become known in due course. It is better to control the timing of an announcement than to let the information leak out.

Most ministers who have to administer discipline will expect to find signs of repentance in the person who has sinned. Each case will have its own complications but, for example, where a deacon has been unfaithful to his wife, the minister would hope to find sorrow and determination to continue the marriage. If this occurs, the deacon would step down from his office (and this would probably require a public announcement) and continue within the church. Support would be given to the man and help to the wife to repair the damage done to their marriage. There would usually need to be a series of meetings held between the couple and their minister to monitor the situation over several months.

If no repentance is shown, then the options become much sharper. In this instance, the deacon, if he wished to continue his liaison with the woman with whom he was having an affair, would find it difficult to continue attending the church, and if she were also a church member, there would be little chance of their staying within the congregation. In these emotionally draining problems the minister often finds him or herself being accused of being too tough or too soft, and it is quite common for church members to take sides in the dispute. If the minister is unwise, the church may split. It is imperative, then, that the facts of the case be discovered by the minister him or herself by asking some very direct questions. Once this has taken place a judgement must be made, and this judgement must consciously weigh up all the factors in the light of Scripture. 1 Corinthians 3–6 shows how Paul acted to break through the paralysis that gripped the congregation at Corinth.

Most ministers will not wish to handle contentious cases requiring discipline on their own and will either ask fellow ministers to help or work with their elders. If there are no elders they will need to recruit reliable church members as witnesses to enquiries. During the process of making enquiries, it is useful to keep an exact record of what was said by whom and, if possible, to minute such records for future reference.

When church life turns nasty, events often move very fast and the congregation will frequently be bewildered by rumours and counter-rumours. Even when the matter is resolved, it will take considerable time to restore the church to its previous state, and it is quite possible that there will be losses both to normal Sunday attendance and to the Sunday offerings. A special church meeting where everything is openly discussed can clear the air, and it is often necessary to have this meeting chaired by someone outside the congregation (a district or diocesan person) who can ensure impartiality.

In the end, the minister must be sure in his or her own mind that the matter has been dealt with as well as possible. If this does not happen, the minister is constantly tempted to destructive self-reproach in the aftermath of the trouble. Wisdom (which does not mean indecisiveness) is required in great quantities.

Questions

1. What leadership style do you use and why?
2. Are your church structures suitable for the main ministerial emphasis of the congregation?
3. Is there anything you should do to ensure that your decision-making meetings are smoothly run?
4. What is the age profile of your congregation? (What percentage of people aged 11–20, 21–30, 31–40, 41–50, 51–60, 61–70 and over 70 have you?)
5. Is your congregation friendly to newcomers? If not, what can you do about this?
6. What most puts members of your congregation off bringing new people to church?
7. Are there matters of discipline you need to attend to?

References

Dunn, J.D.G. (1990), *Jesus, Paul and the Law: studies in Mark and Galatians*, London: SPCK.

Kaldor, P., Bellamy, J., Powell, R., Correy, M. and Castle, K. (1994), *Winds of Change: the experience of church in a changing Australia*, Homebush West: Lancer.

Kay, W.K.and Francis, L.J. (1996), Young Baptists Today, in *Perspectives*, **15**, 5–8.

Rothauge, A. J. (1985), *Sizing Up A Congregation*, New York Episcopal Church.

Explorer setting off to enter the strange world of yoof culture.

Chapter 8

THE MINISTER'S YOUTH WORK

Bible Basis   *Luke 15:11-32*

In this chapter we consider teenagers, youth culture and churches.

The teenager

Mental changes

Huge amounts of effort and time have gone into the study of the changes that take place when we grow up and pass from infancy to adulthood. The mind of the child is different from the mind of the adult and childhood itself is marked by several stages. We are concerned with the transition from the later stages of childhood (roughly from the ages of seven to about twelve) to adolescence.

The mind of the older child is adept at thinking in concrete terms. For instance, if you want to illustrate that a square can be cut into two triangles and that the square and the triangles cover the same area, then it is much easier for children to grasp this if you actually take a square and cut it up in front of them. If you start calculating areas from formulae, the point at issue becomes much more difficult to grasp. So, in the later stages of childhood, children can manipulate physical objects and, in their minds, imagine the manipulation of physical objects, but abstractions are out of their reach.

In adolescence a mental breakthrough occurs. Young people find themselves able to do two things they were not able to do before. First, they can work with abstract concepts (like the ideas of democracy or justice or rights) that cannot be touched and seen. Second, they can think systematically so that, if there are a series of factors responsible for a situation, they can work out what all the possible combinations of factors are and proceed to eliminate them one by one until they arrive at the cause they are looking for (Donaldson, 1978; Bowden, 1979).

These changes enable adolescents for the first time to compete mentally with adults on equal terms. Adolescents may become argumentative and critical as they use their new-found mental capacities to challenge the adult world. They may also become idealistic since, for the first time, they can see how a scheme of abstract concepts can fit together.

Not all these changes occur in all adolescents at the same point and they are most marked in more able young people. Indeed, the development of special intellectual abilities in adolescence is a feature of the age group and, for example, the gap between the most able mathematicians or musicians and the least at the age of fifteen is far greater than it was at the age of nine (Gross, 1992)

Emotional changes

Growing up can be seen as a journey from dependence to independence. The young child is totally dependent on its parents for food, clothing, emotional support, intellectual stimulation, spiritual training – in short, for survival. As the child grows older, it will become more able to look after itself and to relate to its peer group. Eventually the young person will leave home and, ultimately, parents will die and the mature human being copes with life independently of any parental influence. Adolescence is an in-between stage. Here there is a desire for independence and an ability to be independent in many respects but, when crises occur, a tendency to revert to parental support and dependence.

> growing up can be seen as a journey from dependence to independence

The emotional life of adolescence is complicated by the emergence of powerful sexual drives as well as a growth spurt. The sex drives, as we all know, make young people wake up to the attractions of the opposite sex. If you walk into a primary school classroom, boys and girls prefer to sit apart. Within a few years, the situation has completely reversed! The growth spurt ensures that young people change size and shape. Girls tend to reach the growth spurt first so that twelve-year-old girls are bigger than twelve-year-old boys but, by the time mid-adolescence is reached, the boys have caught up and overtaken the girls. Younger girls usually prefer older boys and only subsequently show interest in their exact contemporaries. The growth spurt, however, causes worries about personal appearances and leads teenagers into agonies of self-consciousness or ill-founded bravado. In connection with this survey data show as many as a quarter (27%) of 13–15 year olds have considered suicide (though the actual number of suicides among young people is very small indeed). The reality of the emotional suffering of some young people is seen in the 120,000 cases of self-inflicted harm estimated by the health service each year (Francis and Kay, 1995:53).

Nevertheless we should not exaggerate the universality of the turbulence of adolescence, since at least one study shows that over half (57%) of young people enjoy a 'basically positive, healthy development during early adolescence' and that only 11% have chronic difficulties (Hunt, 1993:393).

Values

In the field of social psychology values are usually seen as enabling us to work out priorities. If we are presented with choices, we opt for a decision that embodies our prime value. For example, if we place a higher value on the environment than personal comfort,

> values are usually seen as enabling us to work out priorities

we are likely to change our lifestyle to accommodate green concerns even if our own comfort suffers.

Young people in Europe tend to value self-expression and personal freedom above any sense of duty (Barker *et al.*, 1993). This leads to an unwillingness to condemn any kind of sexual immorality (though boys react against homosexuality quite strongly) and a general view of religion that it is a private matter and that one religious opinion is as good as another.

Sexual morality among young people is much more permissive than adults sometimes realise. Less than a quarter (24%) of 13–15 year olds in England and Wales believe that it is wrong to have sexual intercourse under the legal age (16 years). This implies that, should the opportunity present itself, as many as three quarters of young people in their mid-teens are unlikely to be restrained from sexual intercourse by moral qualms.

> sexual morality among young people is much more permissive than adults sometimes realise

The position with substance abuse is roughly similar. Only 58% believe that it is wrong to use marijuana and as many as 11% believe that it is *not* wrong to use heroin. The vast majority of young people are likely to have been offered drugs during their adolescence and the reasons for refusing, in most instances, if they do refuse, have little to do with morality (Francis and Kay, 1995).

Attitude toward Christianity

Attitudes are part of everyday conversation. We may say, 'He has a good attitude to work' or 'That boy has an attitude problem' and we understand what is being said. In the 1930s, the American psychologist, L.L. Thurstone, developed a technique for defining and measuring attitudes.

This work was continued in the following decades and statistical sophistication increased. In the 1970s Francis (1976) constructed an attitude toward Christianity scale which has been used in more than a hundred academic studies. In its precise form attitude toward Christianity is both an evaluation and an emotional predisposition. So the person whose attitude toward Christianity is high evaluates Christianity favourably and is emotionally warm towards Christianity. The person with a low attitude to Christianity shows the reverse characteristics.

Studies using the scale show that attitude toward Christianity, among the general school population, declines steadily between the ages of eight and sixteen years, that is, the period from late childhood to mid-adolescence.

> attitude toward Christianity, among the general school population, declines steadily between the ages of eight and sixteen years

Among churchgoing young people a different graph may be drawn. Here the positive attitude of childhood is retained. Churchgoing prevents the erosion of the positive attitude.

The teenager's world

For many teenagers the world is made up of the school, the home, the television and friends.

School

Over 71% of 13–15 year olds are happy at school in England and Wales and 90% like the people they go to school with. Their criticisms fall on the educational process. As many as 35% find school boring and only 42% think that teachers do a good job. As many as 12% think that school is not helping to prepare them for life and 21% are uncertain about this. We have a picture of many young people who like the social process of school but do not think it is delivering the educational goods to them. It is boring and probably will not teach them what will be useful to them in later life.

> Churchgoing prevents the erosion of the positive attitude

There are exceptions to this general picture. About a third of young people like school, succeed there and are favourable to its efforts. At the other end of the spectrum are the 10% who are seriously alienated from school and all it stands for, including the teachers who staff it (Francis and Kay, 1995).

Home

The traditional home in the United Kingdom is a married couple (of the opposite sex) living with their children. 'Since 1972 the proportion of dependent children living in one parent families has tripled; 19% of children lived with just their mother and a further 1% with just their father in 1994 – 95' (*Social Trends* 26, 1996:54). This

> since 1972 the proportion of dependent children living in one parent families has tripled

means that one fifth of dependent children live in one parent families, and this figure is almost exactly paralleled by the proportion of families (22%) in the United Kingdom headed by a lone parent in 1993.

The traditional home is far less common than it used to be and, because the distribution of one parent families is unequal across the country (being highest in Merseyside and Greater London), there are parts of Britain where the single parent has almost become the norm.

Single parenthood may be as a consequence of divorce or cohabitation leading to pregnancy. In 1993 the United Kingdom had the highest divorce rate in the European Community and there were nearly seven times as many divorces in 1993 as there were in 1961. Cohabitation among non-married women aged between 18 and 49 rose to 23 % in 1994 – 95 (*Social Trends 26*, 1996:55).

> in 1993 the United Kingdom had the highest divorce rate in the European Community

When these figures are put together they tell a story of broken relationships and sexual irresponsibility. These children caught up in the crossfire between adults amount to about a fifth of the total of dependent children and, where they lack a father, the consequences for their social development are usually worrying. If the children are boys, they reach their teens beyond the control of their mothers. If they are girls, they are prone to repeat the mistakes of their mothers and produce the next generation of lone parents. Educationally these children may do poorly at school, and this means that they are then condemned to low paid jobs or unemployment.

Even in traditional two-parent homes, the story is not guaranteed to have a happy ending. When asked whether they find it helpful to talk about their problems with their fathers, less than a third of 13–15 year olds (31%) agree. The mother is far more popular in this respect. Over half (51%) find they can talk to their mothers. More alarming is the statistic showing that over half of girls (56%) find their fathers positively unhelpful, and this compares with over a third (36%) of boys.

The relationships between parents and teenagers, especially when teenagers have problems, are not sweet. A very significant number of young people are either clashing with their parents or unable to confide in them. These figures are more healthy when they focus only on church-going young people but not much more so (Francis and Kay, 1995).

Television

Figures show that about a quarter of 13–15 year olds in England and Wales watch more than four hours a day. These young people are more inclined to approve of anti-social acts than those who relate to real human beings. Social isolation caused by television addiction suggests a desire for stimulation without any corresponding concern for friends or family, a recipe for pain in future relationships (Francis, 1996).

The telecommunications revolution has multiplied television sets so that large numbers of young people have a TV in their bedrooms where, presumably, they can watch whatever they like at any hour of the day or night. The arrival of satellite and cable television multiplies choice and gives purely pornographic films easy access to the unsuspecting household.

Extreme libertarians argue that artistic free expression should allow them to make and broadcast films containing any kind of violence or sexual explicitness. They argue that there is no link between what is seen on television and human behaviour. This argument is false. There is good research evidence that the visual media influence behaviour, and this is underlined every time a successful advertising campaign persuades people to buy a product they have only recently heard about (Eysenck and Nias, 1979).

> there is good research evidence that the visual media influence behaviour

Television broadcasting now takes place nearly twenty-four hours a day in most western countries. It has fragmented and targeted on niche markets as well as the broad streams of popular culture. Tabloid television occupies the prime slots and niche television, at less popular times, appeals to minorities, whether ethnic, opera-loving or homosexual.

Television output is to a great extent influenced by a battle for audience share: the BBC which is funded by the licence payer must justify its licence fee and ITV, which is funded by advertising, must gain viewers for its sponsors. In the United States fifteen minutes of advertising occurs in each hour; in Britain advertising runs to about half this. Since young people have money to spend, and since they rarely have family or other responsibilities, their buying power is enormous. Clothes, fashion accessories, music, holidays, cars and magazines can all operate entirely from the funds of young people. Commentators now talk about 'the fashion industry' or 'the music industry' since this is the best way to describe them.

Young people, unaware of the commercial forces at work behind the facade of fashion and trends, are easily persuaded that unless they own *this* brand of shoe or *that* type of deodorant, their chances of success with the opposite sex are negligible.

Friends

These are an important support system. As young people move from
the orbit of parents to the world of work, friends function a little like
an alternative family. Young people who join gangs almost always
have no families to off-set the life of the gang, and the gang leader is a
sort of father (or in the case of female gangs mother) figure. But for
the majority of young people, friends simply are an unorganised social
group sharing interests and aims.

As many as two-thirds (67%) of young people say that they 'often hang
around with their friends doing
nothing in particular', though the
function of friendships among
males and females is different.
While three quarters of girls (78%)
say they find it helpful to talk
about their problems with close friends, the corresponding figure for boys
is less than half (45%). Girls use the advice of friends to help them solve
their problems, while boys tend to talk less and act more (Francis and
Kay, 1995).

> girls use the advice of friends
> to help them solve their
> problems

Youth culture

Those who work with young people all the time compare youth work
with cross-cultural mission. They speak of youth culture's 'anarchic
materialism' where possessions must be purchased even though the
value and meaning of those possessions may be contradictory: a 'save
the whale T-shirt' is worn alongside a pair of leather boots to beg the
question why whales are more special than cows. They speak of the
visual nature of culture, full of images and icons, that shouts in style
while lacking any substance. Each company has its 'logo', each musical
fashion (funk, rock, or whatever) has its corresponding visual signifier
(an ear ring, a nose ring, a tattoo, a leather jacket, a designer label item
of clothing) and each drug scene its preferred graffiti, its own slang.

Ethical relativism reigns. Every opinion is right. One man can
believe that Elvis Presley is alive
and another that a crystal has
healing powers; one woman can
believe she is a reincarnation of
a foreign princess and another that she can detect the ley lines where

> ethical relativism reigns

ancient religion was practised; one man can proclaim on television that he is really King Arthur (and changes his name to back up his claim) and another that everyone has an aura detectable only to the psychically sensitive that reveals their real character; one girl can trust horoscopes as a sure-fire way of finding happiness in love and one boy can put blind faith in science as the royal road to truth. Many young people have no idea how to evaluate these claims and accept them along with the voting system, football matches and computers. They are just there, part of the social landscape.

From an historical perspective the 1990s young people are the grandchildren of the 1960s and often come from two generations of dysfunctional adults. The least successful of these young people feel alienated from society: they have enough money to be apathetic about politics and not enough confidence or knowledge to demonstrate against government policies as the young of 1968 did on the campus of Berkeley and on the streets of Paris. But the sense of mission is heightened by the general ignorance of Christianity. Sunday school has almost vanished. Churchgoing has declined and, as a result, many young people, despite or because of the religious education they receive in school, have little conception of the contents of the New Testament and a hazy, but often militant, notion about the theory of evolution. Further details of the contours of youth culture are given in Francis, Kay, Kerbey and Fogwill (1995).

Legal considerations relevant to youth worth

The Home Office in 1993 published *Safe from Harm* in which it was stated that 'every voluntary organisation should consider whether to adopt a brief written statement setting out its policy on safeguarding the welfare of the children with whom it works. The policy should state clearly the duty of all those employed by or involved in the organisation to prevent the physical, sexual or emotional abuse of all children with whom they come into contact.'

The Children Act of 1989 has already stressed the principle that the welfare of the child is of paramount importance in all circumstances.

It is legally permissible to enquire about past convictions for criminal offences of anyone applying for work with children, since this work is exempt from the provision of Section 4(2) of the Rehabilitation of Offenders Act 1974, by virtue of the Rehabilitation of Offenders Act 1974 (Exceptions) Order 1975.

For these legal reasons, youth workers should be asked to complete a declaration regarding disclosure of criminal records and civil court orders and, if the selection procedure identifies circumstances in which the welfare of a child has previously been put at risk by a candidate for youth work, consultation with the Department of Health should be made.

> it is legally permissible to enquire about past convictions for criminal offences of anyone applying for work with children

Further references must be sought, indicating that the candidate is not automatically debarred from the appointment.

By taking these precautions, churches are not only protecting their children and young people from abuse but also protecting themselves from public condemnation in the terrible event that things go wrong.

Mission to youth

Christian mission to youth from a congregation has two aspects. First, there is provision for children who have grown up in the church, understand its message, pray, share the faith of their parents and are trying to live for Jesus. Second, there is mission to the unconverted majority whose parents do not attend church and who, to a greater or lesser extent, share the characteristics found in the wider youth culture. They may be television addicts, or have been offered and taken drugs, be sexually experienced, unsure of their own identity, caught up in the fashion or music industry, performing poorly at school and erratically bouncing between dependence of adults and macho independence.

The mission to the first group of young people is carried out by the traditional youth group. Here young people are offered a mixture of social or sporting activities in the context of overall Christian teaching. The youth group may adopt a programme alternating social activities with evenings of bible study or it may try to add bible study and prayer on the end of every youth evening. These patterns all have the aim of keeping the interest of young people and allowing the minister to get to know them individually while, at the same time, giving biblical teaching appropriate to the temptations and pressures faced by young people. To this end, youth camps are often especially successful. Here young people can enjoy outdoor fun and games during the day and, in the evening, worship and listen to good preaching. Similarly, the occasional youth rally, often with the appeal of Christian rock music, can enliven a winter programme and serve to attract young people on the edge of the church.

The mission to the raw recruits of secular youth culture is a much more difficult proposition, especially when it is combined with an attempt to provide a youth programme for children from Christian homes. Various models are being tried. For example, Oxford Youth Works has pioneered an 'incarnational' model which operates by befriending young people without trying to bring them quickly into Christian meetings and services. Some Christian youth clubs are run on lines similar to secular youth clubs, but with a hidden Christian agenda. Similarly, Christian Union meetings in school, if they are run by teachers or ministers entirely on a voluntary basis, can attract unchurched young people and nurture them through Scripture Union booklets of daily bible readings and similar schemes.

Preaching to young people must be direct and speak to their concerns. It is important for the preacher to try to understand not only the world of young people but also the physical and psychological processes with which young people are caught up. They may have genuine questions about sex or drugs (not simply designed to embarrass the minister), and their intellectual enquiries about God, Jesus and the bible are likely to be a mixture between the sharp and the naive. Their assumptions are likely to be heavily infused by the ethical relativism of their culture and the materialism common to western culture as a whole. They may also have an almost mystical belief in the power of science and technology coupled with an awesome ignorance of science's branches and first principles. So far as Christianity goes, their attitude, if they are non-churchgoers, is likely to be negative which, in practice, amounts to indifference.

It is helpful to show the reasonableness of Christianity to young people. Many will respond to the evidence for the resurrection of Christ and the reliability of the bible, which have never been presented to them before. Many will appreciate the 'argument from design' showing the order in the universe and its implication that there is a Creator responsible for that order. Others will begin to grapple with the sufferings in the world, and may come to appreciate that the existence of human free will almost inevitably co-incides with the misuse of that free will, and therefore of human suffering.

Sometimes the presentation of Christianity becomes simply a presentation of Christ. Here the various needs of young people are met.

> sometimes the presentation of Christianity becomes simply a presentation of Christ

Those who are looking for excitement, danger and challenge will find it in the call to follow Christ wherever he may lead, whether to missionary work overseas or to the local tower block. Other young people, whose lives may have been shaken by emotional upsets at home, are looking for love and security, and that too is found in Christ. The promise of Christ's continuing love has an appeal for both sexes, especially for those who have been betrayed in previous relationships. And, to all young people, Christ offers an opportunity for a new start where, in the knowledge that God cares for them, they may find self-respect and self-acceptance.

The integration of young people into the life of a congregation depends not only on the individual young person but also on the kind of congregation in view. The Free Church congregation with popular music, a relaxed preaching style and ordinary clothes has an advantage here over high church variants. The importance of allowing young people to be full participants in what is going on must be stressed. If young people feel that the church is being run entirely for middle-aged people, they will feel put off and unhappy. The minister has the task of involving both young and old without offending either group.

Although there has been discussion about the possibility of 'youth churches' (Francis, Kay, Kerbey and Fogwill, 1995), these do not seem to be necessary where older people are willing to unbend. Likewise, the 'youth pastor' or 'youth minister', familiar in the United States, is becoming more common in Britain despite the financial restrictions which prevent the funding of two full-time ministers in one congregation, but this need not mean that there are bound to be two mini-congregations in practice. Youth pastors take part in services for the whole church and, in this way, the young people feel that their voice is heard and that they have a direct line into the decision-making part of the church.

Questions

1. How well are young people integrated into your congregation? Are they given enough to do? Are there opportunities for them to grow in their Christian lives? Are older people in the congregation unfriendly with young people? Are young people unfriendly to older people?
2. Are your youth meetings appropriate to the current generation of young people?
3. Examine the parables of Jesus to see how many young people are in them. What does this show you?
4. Compose a talk or sermon addressing the concerns of young people.

References

Bowden, M.A. (1979), *Piaget*, Glasgow, Fontana Paperbacks.

Barker, D., Halman, L. and Vloet, A. (1993), *The European Values Study 1981–1990*, London/The Netherlands: European Values Group.

Donaldson, M. (1978), *Children's Minds*, London: Fontana Press.

Eysenck, H.J. and Nias, D.K.B. (1979), *Sex, Violence and the Media*, London: Scientific Book Club.

Francis, L.J. (1976), An enquiry into the concept 'readiness for religion', University of Cambridge, PhD thesis.

Francis, L.J. (1996), The Socio-Psychological Profile of the Teenage Television Addict, paper read at Fitzwilliam College, Cambridge, 13 July, 1996.

Francis L.J. and Kay, W.K. (1995), *Teenage Religion and Values*, Leominster: Gracewing.

Francis, L.J., Kay, W.K., Kerbey A. and Fogwill, O. (1995) (eds), *Fast-Moving Currents in Youth Culture*, Oxford: Lynx Communications.

Gross, R.D. (1992), *Psychology: the Science of Mind and Behaviour*, London: Hodder and Stoughton.

Hunt, M. (1993), *The Story of Psychology*, New York: Doubleday.

Social Trends 26 (1996), London: HMSO.

Chapter 9

THE MINISTER'S DENOMINATION

Bible Basis　　*Acts 15*
　　　　　　　　John 17

There were no denominations in the New Testament because denominations developed historically, often by emphasising a particular doctrine. For this reason, in putting a biblical perspective on today's
relationship between a minister and his or her denomination, it is
necessary to argue from general Scriptural principles rather from than
precise examples captured in the pages of the New Testament itself.

The nearest the New Testament church comes to the formation of
denominations occurs either
when two apostles found separate
networks of congregations or
when congregations contain high
proportions of people from Jewish or Gentile backgrounds.[6] In
practice the two possible divisions
between churches existed together: Peter went to preach to
largely Jewish communities and
founded congregations, at least at

> the nearest the New
> Testament church comes to
> the formation of
> denominations occurs
> when two apostles found
> separate networks of
> congregations

the beginning, that were tinged by Jewish religious thought and outlook, and Paul went to preach to largely Gentile communities and

---

[6.] The tribal nature of Israel also offers an illustration of denominations. Each tribe
had its own elders and its own land and the nation was at its best when the tribes co-
operated. The tribes resemble modern denominations, though we should not push
this analogy too far!

founded congregations that were influenced by Gentile outlooks and lifestyles. The church in Jerusalem tended to be legalistic, and the church in Corinth tended to be libertarian.

The clash between the two sorts of churches is implied by the letter to the Galatians and brought into the open during the Council of Jerusalem recorded in Acts 15. At the Council, the extreme Jewish faction argued that it was necessary to keep the law of Moses to be saved and that any Gentile who, while believing that Jesus was the Messiah, refused to obey the Mosaic law could not be saved. On the other side of the argument Paul argued that it was by faith in Jesus, and faith alone, that human beings were saved and that the Mosaic law never had, and never could, properly remove human sin. The arguments were deep, but the Council eventually reached a solution that was acceptable to everyone.

One implication to be drawn from this Council is that Christians with deep differences should be able to sit down together and look for agreement.

There were further divergencies between the congregations of the Jerusalem area and those in Greece. The congregations in and around Jerusalem were poor, while those of Greece were, in the main, relatively prosperous. So Paul organised a collection and money was sent from the richer parts of the church to the poorer parts (1 Cor 16:1). The two parts saw themselves as belonging together.

One implication to be drawn from this is that congregations in richer parts of the world should help congregations in poorer parts of the world.

But what of relationships within existing denominations today?

The minister and denominational colleagues

In theory ministers in the same denomination should have a great deal in common. They should share the doctrinal views that make their denomination distinct and they should relate in a similar way to the next level in the denominational hierarchy.

Most denominations of any size have a regional gathering of their ministers at regular intervals. It is here that inter-congregational events can be planned and older ministers can encourage younger ones. In practice regional gatherings are not always happy occasions, and we consider this negative scenario first. Factions, disagreements, willful personalities, financial concerns and over-talkative individuals who commandeer the agenda are all likely to appear.

Ministers can become disillusioned about the denomination they belong to. They know that, if they leave their denomination, they are going to find the same problems elsewhere and, because they know their own denomination so well, they despair of its ever changing. In addition, they are aware that, in some respects, they are tied into their denomination. Their house may be a manse, their pension may be held in a denominational fund and their children may be at a church school. They sometimes feel that they must simply soldier on till retirement.

Such an assessment of the situation calls for an answer. The demoralised minister will demoralise other ministers, congregations will dwindle and a spiral of decline will twirl downwards. What can be done?

The successful minister may be tempted to retreat to his or her own congregation where things are going well. Here there may be life and growth and a real sense of progress. What all too often happens is that the successful minister, who could make a difference to ministerial gatherings, opts out thinking that time and energy are better spent elsewhere.

And this is the crux of this chapter. To be involved or not to be involved, that is the question. Some years ago Jack Hayford, the author of the song 'Majesty', faced this issue (Hayford, 1982:36f). He was ministering to a congregation in Van Nuys, California, belonging to the ICFG (International Church of the Foursquare Gospel) denomination and when he took over in 1969, there were 18 people in attendance. Over the course of several years the congregation grew to 6,000 people. He had no need of the denomination's support or advice. He was big enough to go alone. He decided instead to remain with the church's denominational roots and to continue to contribute financially to the denomination's running costs. This was a decision many ministers would have choked on. After all, what is the point in giving good money for the sake of administration and bureaucracy? But Hayford's point was that this was a matter of honour as well as spirituality. The denomination had helped the congregation when it was weak, now it was the congregation's privilege to help the denomination when the positions were reversed.

> to be involved or not to be involved, that is the question

There is a view, preached from time to time, that denominations are a disgrace to the unity of the church and that, until denominations are abolished, the prayer of Jesus in John 17 can never be answered. This is clearly not a position Hayford would accept. But is the condemnation of denominations on the grounds of teaching about church unity really based in the text of the New Testament?

Jesus prays that the church will be protected 'so that they may be one as we are one' (Jn 17:11). The unity of the church is to match the unity within the Trinity, a unity which is also a plurality. Yes, Christian doctrine teaches that there is one God, but one God in Three Persons. Such a prayer does not amount to the removal of all distinctions between congregations or groups of Christians. Rather it asks for a harmonious loving relationship while permitting, even enjoining, distinctions within the Christian community to reflect distinctions with the Godhead.

A similar conclusion may be drawn from Ephesians 4 where there is enormous stress on the common experience and beliefs of Christians. There is one body, one Spirit, one hope, one Lord, one faith, one baptism, one God, as well as an equal stress on the diversities of Christian ministry – apostles, prophets, evangelists, pastors and teachers. The unity is possible because of the diversity of ministry, and the diversity of ministry leads

> such a prayer does not amount to the removal of all distinctions between congregations or groups of Christians

to further unity – that 'we all reach a unity in the faith and in the knowledge of the Son of God' (v.13). The New Testament allows for the complex reality of the Christian life. It does not give us a cheap ecumenical tract but, instead, endorses an expensive (in terms of time and effort) set of relationships infused by the love of Christ.

We take the view, then, that the minister should support his or her denomination without surrendering to denominationalism, which is an attitude akin to that found among football supporters who can see no good in any other team in the league. Denominationalism is 'party spirit', tribalism, even sectarianism, and has no place within gatherings called in Jesus' name.

Where the ministerial gathering is a pleasure to attend, relationships with the denomination present no problem to the minister. He or she should find, in these settings, colleagues who precisely understand the ups and downs of church life. In general, ministerial gatherings are happiest when they focus on practical and spiritual issues (how should youth work be improved? Is the minister's devotional life what it should be?) and reduce the amount of business they deal with.

The minister and the denominational hierarchy

Historically, denominational hierarchies were set up for different reasons. Most draw their inspiration from the New Testament and see the regional minister (a bishop for an Anglican, a superintendent for a Methodist) as being provided for pastoral care, to minister to the minister. The bishop in some strands of tradition may be seen as a guardian of doctrinal orthodoxy and administrator of ecclesiastical discipline, and there can be a tension between the hierarchy's various roles.

The minister of a local congregation will be expected to call in the hierarchy when in trouble, and the hierarchy will normally be keen that their ministers are spiritually and mentally healthy. There can be friction between a minister and the bishop or superintendent but, if this is so, the minister should recall that 'promotion' within a denomination is usually a matter of peer group recognition. In other words men or women rise to have charge over other ministers because they are valued by their

> men or women rise to have charge over other ministers because they are valued by their contemporaries

contemporaries. The minister who finds him or herself in dispute with a senior minister must therefore be prepared to give the benefit of the doubt to the senior minister.

The example of David's relationship with Saul provides an Old Testament example of what happens when junior and senior colleagues clash. David knew that he was to succeed Saul as king, but he made no attempt to assassinate Saul. He let events take their course and trusted God.

In the New Testament a dispute takes place between Paul and Barnabas. Barnabas begins as the senior of the two men (he is a Christian several years before Paul's conversion) and Paul owes his acceptance by the Jerusalem church to Barnabas' initiative. The two men travel together on the first missionary journey and then disagree over the arrangements for the next journey and go their separate ways (Acts 15:37,39). Yet there is no feud and Paul always mentions Barnabas with sympathy and respect.

The minister and denominational co-operation

There may be practical difficulties for a minister who is invited to take part in a town-wide collaboration of churches at the same time as commitments to denominational events require support. This dilemma, like many others of ministerial life, is one of priorities. Most ministers try to work out a balance between competing demands and they may find that, over several years, this balance has to be adjusted one way or the other.

A judgement must be made. We suggest that the minister needs to ask which of several possible courses of action will be most beneficial to the congregation he or she serves. After considering the needs of the congregation, the minister should then add in what he or she would prefer. Big occasions, where members of small congregations can be part of a large-scale Christian event, are often exciting and transmit enthusiasm into the day-to-day life of the church. The minister, who may find his or her own needs met in a smaller gathering of fellow ministers, may receive less benefit from the large-scale event. This is where the needs of the congregation take precedence. The main thing to avoid is attendance for the sake of attendance since this causes ministers (and their congregations) to be busy without achieving anything.

Mission, whether this involves the collection of money or articles for short-term aid or long-term financial commitment to overseas projects, is frequently rooted in denominational structures. Research (Francis and Kay, 1995:70f) has shown that Christian young people are concerned about Third World poverty. Ministers, if they are not careful, can simply see giving money to missions as a way of impoverishing the local church's bank account. There are two equal and opposite errors to avoid here.

First, it is foolish to idealise the work of missions to the extent that local needs are ignored. There is no point in having a big collection for the poor of a Third World country if poverty on the door step is overlooked. There may be poor members of the local congregation who need help, and if so, they should be helped.

Second, it is foolish to ignore the work of missions because the church needs to buy a new tea urn. There must be a sense, encouraged by preaching, that the church in the wealthier part of the world has a responsibility for its members abroad. The best way to make this responsibility a reality is to invite representatives of charitable organisations (especially their own Missions or Social Action Sections) to speak to the church. They will come and show videos and let the church see what can be done by consistent giving. Indeed, the minister would be wise to have a policy of being involved with a few charitable organisations with whom personal contact can be established. This way it is possible for the congregation to gain a general idea of progress that can be made in projects that can be adopted.

The minister's conference, congress or synod

Most denominations call a big ministerial meeting together each year. This meeting may, in some denominations, include laity (or non-ordained people) as a way of widening representation. Most years the decisions or statements made by such big meetings have no great impact on local congregations, and there is a temptation for the minister to leave the conference business to those who enjoy the cut and thrust of debate.

It is helpful to distinguish between the different kinds of decisions conferences may make.

There may be:

- fundamental decisions (e.g. the ordination of women in the Anglican church);
- structural decisions (e.g. introducing a regionalisation in Assemblies of God);
- administrative decisions (e.g. which only change the way things are done).

We would argue that ministers who confuse these separate categories of decision become unnecessarily anxious or angry. Structural and administrative decisions leave the denomination's heart untouched and it is perfectly reasonable to make changes so as to allow the churches to adapt to a changing world. The vital debates concern fundamental decisions and, though there is room for dis-

> the minister has a perfect right to put his or her point of view to the conference but, having done this, should abide by the decision which has been made

agreement about exactly when a decision becomes fundamental, the principle is clear enough.

The minister has a perfect right to put his or her point of view to the conference but, having done this, should abide by the decision which has been made. Once the decision-making process is accepted, and after the minister has contributed to that process, he or she is bound by whatever is decided. To do otherwise is to imply that the decision-making process is only worthwhile because it agrees with personal opinion.

Questions

1. What are the practical benefits of belonging to a denomination?
2. How would you decide priorities between commitment to denominational demands and town-wide (or city-wide) collaboration involving many denominations?
3. What are the dangers of denominationalism?

References

Hayford, J. W. (1982), *The Church on the Way*, Grand Rapids: Zondervan.

Francis, L. J. and Kay, W. K. (1995), *Teenage Religion and Values*, Leominster: Gracewing

Chapter 10

THE MINISTER'S COMMUNITY

Bible Basis   *Matthew 5:13,14*
              James 2:1-7
              Romans 13:1-6

In or out of touch?

Some congregations rise above their communities like islands. While the community, urban or rural, multi-racial or mono-racial, pursues its own fashions and struggles, observes its own sporting and civic rituals and follows its own stars and leaders, the church is detached in another cultural world. Here, 'the language of Zion' is spoken, a language that is incomprehensible to the average watcher of TV soaps who, arriving on the fringes of the church, is immediately estranged.

Other congregations are not so much islands as part of their communities. The language of the pulpit is also the language of the newspapers. The music of worship is locatable somewhere in the musical culture of the day. In General Booth's famous words, 'Why should the devil have all the best tunes?' The clothing of the church is the smart-casual clothing of leisure. Anyone walking from the community into the church at least understands what is said, even if, at first, they do not believe it.

The early church certainly spoke the language of its day. The New Testament was written in *koine* or common Greek and the theological terminology of the New Testament adapted and adopted the language of the streets. Even so basic a term as the word 'church' was in use in Greek society and referred to a civic assembly before it was given an exclusively Christian meaning. There were few cultural barriers to cross for the new Christian. The clothing worn in church was no different from the robe or toga that was the normal wear of men and women throughout the Roman world. Interesting recent historical detective work has been done on the first urban Christians and it has been shown that the trade guilds were an important network by which the faith travelled. Itinerant workers would find it relatively easy to introduce their colleagues to the Christian congregation (Meeks, 1983).

> the early church certainly spoke the language of its day

The changes required by the new convert to Christianity were great enough and affected lifestyle, outlook and behaviour, but these were changes rooted in theology and not in culture. It is unreasonable to overlay Christianity today with a class culture and then to expect new converts to see the pure theology of the New Testament. What is needed is the theology of the New Testament in the language of the 20th century.

The structure of the community

Cities

We have spoken of the local community as if it is obviously signposted. But, in reality, this is not so. The community is largely determined by patterns of housing. The wealthy have a choice of housing while the poor are confined to the cheaper end of the market. Consequently social zoning occurs, and in many western cities the wealthy moved to the outskirts of cities and away from the business or industrial areas. Cities came to be arranged in concentric rings, with the poorest in the centre and the richest on the outside.

> the community is largely determined by patterns of housing

This pattern has in recent years, to some extent, broken down and it is now not distance so much as travelling time that determines the zones. Urban clearways, ringroads and transport systems bring parts of the city that used to be seen as unconnected closer together. The city may develop more than one centre and, when the outer part of the city becomes too far from the business blocks, the rich may reclaim the old inner city houses – as has happened in parts of London.

What has remained the same, though, is that immigrants to the city tend to cluster together in 'villages' or 'ghettos' simply because the family structures that make immigration possible offer much more effective support in close-knit proximity. Immigrants tend to be younger and their birth rates are higher than those longer established in the city. This eventually leads to pressure on the housing stock and further migration may then take place. While this happens, it is common for young professionals, perhaps from higher income families, to compete for the cheaper accommodation with poorer, older people. A mixture of poor immigrant workers and young, mobile professionals is then found, and this is a common location for many older churches that were originally built for the wealthy families who have now moved elsewhere. The whole process of urban change has been well studied and is helpful to city ministers (Hall, 1981; Carter, 1995).

The minister is advised to analyse the local area, perhaps by visiting the reference section of the local library and making enquiries there. What do government census data say? Are there any plans for new roads or buildings? Are the schools growing or closing? Do people move on from the area after a few years? What sort of jobs, age group, ethnicity and expectations do the local people have? A brief analysis will enable the minister to decide what sort of priorities to set for the immediate future and what may be needed in a few years time. It may also enable the church to work out where the natural leadership of the community is. There may be a residents' association or a Working Men's Club or a Community Centre where people gather and the church would be wise to relate to these secular structures with a view to collaboration.

If the area attracts particular kinds of people (young professionals living in two room apartments, for example), then the church should be designed to cater for their needs. Perhaps the times of services need changing. Perhaps the worship style needs altering. If there are poorer migrant workers in the district as well, then the church should also focus on them and become a place where the two types of resident may meet and interact.

If the area is a residential one where young couples bring up families, then the church must adapt to these needs by ensuring that children are catered for. If the area is non-residential, and people travel in to church by car, then a transport system must be arranged. Ideally, however, people should be able to walk into the church from the street and feel welcome.

Towns

A town, from the sociological point of view, is not simply smaller than a city. Its pattern of residence is less complicated, and its governing body is closer to the people. The old market town is situated within walking distance of villages and the farmers used to bring their livestock to the town square to sell them on market day. The town hall was built on the side of the square and local government administered from the council chamber. A congregation in this sort of town would expect to attract people to worship from the villages, and the link between village and town would be strong enough to enable most people, even if they lived in the villages, to identify with the town. Only where the villages function as dormitories for a city some miles away would village life predominate and the village church become important (Francis, 1996).

New towns in Britain were constructed according to a plan that kept industrial or business estates separate from housing estates. People could travel round the town on a ringroad from housing estate to housing estate and only needed to go into the town centre on major shopping expeditions. Each housing estate was built with small local shops and usually had a pub, post office, school and a church (newly built) as well. Attempts were sometimes made to mix private and council housing. Local government was still administered from the town hall, one of the older buildings in the centre.

Congregations formed on housing estates could either appeal to the people on the estate or, because travel is easy, to denominational loyalties. In practice this urban structure has proved to be ideal for large multi-congregation churches, that is, for churches which, under one leadership, operate a congregation on most of the estates in the town. The pattern of church attendance in new towns is therefore usually different from that found in market towns, and ministers who recognise this are saved false starts by trying to build churches against the natural flow of people's journeys.

> the pattern of church attendance in new towns is therefore usually different from that found in market towns

In both kinds of town the social distance between people and local government is relatively small and open to church influence.

Salt

Jesus said to his disciples 'You are the salt of the earth' (Mt 5:13). In the ancient world salt was a preservative. There was no refrigeration and, to keep meat from decaying, it was dried and salted. After salting the meat would keep for long periods of time. Even in the 19th century, British naval vessels carried barrels of salted beef on long voyages as a staple diet for sailors.

The salt of the earth is a preservative. Without it, the earth is corrupted, crawling with maggots and only fit for throwing away. The church is placed on the earth to fight corruption and, if the salt loses its saltiness, it has no useful function.

Salt acts on whatever it contacts. It is no good just putting salt in the same room as meat. An old farmer explained how, during the 1939–45 war, he used to keep a side of pork in his cellar. It was an afternoon's hard work to rub the salt into the meat until it was ready to be put away for the win-

> Salt acts on whatever it contacts. It is no good just putting salt in the same room as meat.

ter. It must be rubbed in till the salt permeates the meat. This means the church must be in contact with, and permeate, society if society is to receive any benefit.

In European cities, the church rarely affects the spheres of commerce and law. The church works where it can, but the millions who come and go, and the councillors and officials who run the city are not often touched by the good news of Christ. Yet, the church can make an impact. Roger Forster tells the story of how the Ichthus Fellowship in London joined with other evangelical churches to challenge a local council on issues of moral concern arising from the council's policies. In addition they aired the subject more widely by leafletting thousands of homes in the borough, explaining the council's policies to voters and their objections to them. At first the local council ignored the churches but as the issues were raised more widely in the local and national press, things began to change. Over the next couple of years, extremists and their policies on the council were replaced by moderates, and good relationships with the churches were restored. (Kay and Shenton, 1993).

In market towns, where the local government is relatively close to the people, there are usually many opportunities to ensure that corrupt decisions are challenged. It is possible to attend debates, to write to the local press and to make the Christian voice heard, especially if several churches combine together.

In new towns, the same opportunities exist. The real battles often take place when commercial interests seem to dictate one course of action and Christian integrity dictates another. But, the saltiness of Christianity is not necessarily a matter of campaigns – if this were so Christianity would turn into another pressure group lobbying for social or ecological causes. Christianity presses for integrity in government. Is public money properly spent? Are there concealed diversions of funds for improper purposes?

Romans 13:1 teaches that 'the authorities that exist have been established by God'. Civic government is God-given and something to be thankful for; these are implications from words of Scripture written during the pagan Roman empire. The thrust of Christian efforts in the sphere of local government must be (whatever Liberation Theology may say) to improve and not to overthrow.

Liberation Theologians teach, on the basis of the rescue of the Israelite slaves from Egypt, that the church must first work in the political realm and then in the spiritual realm (O'Collins and Farrugia, 1991). But this is to misunderstand the Scriptural order. When the spiritual is correct, the political will be corrected. In the Old Testament, it was the idolatrous king Ahab who stole Naboth's vineyard (1 Kings 21). Because he was idolatrous, Ahab neglected the covenant that guaranteed every family its land. Even the rescue of the Israelite slaves from Egypt only succeeded because Moses was obedient to God, and the rescue took place through God's power and not by political campaigning.

Every so often Christians ask whether there could be a Christian political party. The idea sounds wonderful and the voting muscle of the church would then, it is claimed, produce a political programme that would usher in peace and righteousness. Unfortunately this idea is dashed to pieces on the rocks of Christian disagreement. It has proved almost impossible to find a political, as opposed to a moral, platform on which Christians can unite. The bible itself does not advocate one form of government rather than another. The bible is concerned for justice in government and for care of the poor and underprivileged by whatever system might be in place. The attempt to work out a manifesto for Christian politics on the basis of the law of Moses is untenable. The law of Moses has been superseded by the new covenant.

Light

Jesus said 'Let your light shine before men, that they may see your good deeds and praise your Father in heaven' (Mt 5:16). If the church is to give light, it must do good.

A false choice may be offered to ministers: either propagate a 'social Gospel' or really preach the Gospel. Yet the two go together. The love of Christ prompts both. There is a need to feed the hungry *and* to preach the Gospel to them; a need to visit the prisoners *and* to preach the Gospel to them; a need to visit those who are ill in hospital *and* to preach the Gospel to them.

The practice of doing good is a major theme of the early church. Dorcas was known to help the poor by making clothes for widows (Acts 9:39), the church in Antioch sent financial help to the church in Jerusalem (Acts 11:29), the apostles James, Peter and John were concerned that the Gentile church being planted by Paul should 'remember the poor' (Gal 2:10), Paul in one of his final letters tells Timothy to 'command those who are rich... to be rich in good deeds and to be generous and willing to share' (1 Tim 6:18) and James says that acceptable religion looks after orphans and widows (Js 1:27).

There are five practical reasons for doing good. First, 'It is God's will that by doing good you should silence the ignorant talk of foolish men' (1 Pet 2:15). In other words, the charitable acts of the church shame critics of Christianity into silence. Even today, when we read the attacks made upon the Salvation Army by T. H. Huxley, the populariser of Darwinianism, Huxley seems petty, unfeeling and morally repugnant (Collier, 1997:172f). Second, the charitable acts of the church reflect the character of the God to whom the church bears witness. God's love for human beings flows from an unconditional love for the whole human race and, by

> the charitable acts of the church reflect the character of God

doing good, the church makes this truth a reality. Third, if God loves human beings, then it makes sense to believe that the church will try to relieve whatever suffering it might find. Fourth, if Christ himself did good, and if Christ is the authentic example for all Christians to follow, then it is logical that Christians should demonstrate their discipleship by doing good whenever they can. Fifth, the charitable acts of the church prepare people to accept the Gospel. If Christians behave like this, then it is possible to believe that Christ really died for sinners.

✍ Questions

1. What are the barriers between your congregation and your community?
2. How can your congregation act as salt? Think of some practical steps which might be fitted into a short-term plan.
3. How can your congregation act as light? Are there obvious areas of darkness where Christian light needs to shine?

References

Carter, H. (1995), *The Study of Urban Geography*, London: Arnold.

Collier, R. (1977), *The General Next To God*, Glasgow: Wm Collins and Sons.

Francis, L.J. (1996), *Church Watch: Christianity in the Countryside,* London: SPCK.

Hall, P. (ed) (1981), *The Inner City in Context*, London: Heinemann.

Kay, W.K. and Shenton, W. (1993), *Harvest Now*, Nottingham: Lifestream Publications.

Meeks, W.A. (1983), *The First Urban Christians*, Yale: Yale University Press.

O'Collins, G. and Farrugia E.G. (1991), *A Concise Dictionary of Theology*, London: HarperCollins.

Part 2:

COUNSELLING

Chapter 11

APPROACHES TO COUNSELLING

Bible Basis   *Isaiah 9:6*
John 14:16–18
Romans 8
1 Thessalonians 2:7,11

Counselling, in recent years, has become a massive and complex subject where a variety of systems and approaches are advocated. It has been estimated that there are over 400 different approaches to counselling currently in use (Palmer, Dainow and Milner, 1996:1). Professional qualifications in counselling are in the process of settling down and it is still not clear whether the subject belongs with one or other branches of psychology or psychiatry or is a subject on its own and not under the umbrella of another discipline.

While counselling itself is seeking to reach agreement about its methods and parameters, the relationship between pastoral theology and counselling is bound to remain fluid.[7]

In this chapter we outline three purely humanistic approaches to counselling and criticise them. We then show how Christian counsellors have adapted these humanistic approaches. Finally, we present one biblical approach to counselling.

Humanistic approaches to counselling

Behaviouristic counselling

This method use the ideas of Burrhus F. Skinner (1904–90) and his

---

[7.] The Clinical Pastoral Education (CPE) movement was established in the United States in the 1930s and is well organised and accredited. Its impact on Britian was until recently relatively slight.

followers. In this approach the inner thoughts and feeling of the client are ignored in favour of a concentration on behaviour. Behaviour is said to be formed by external stimuli rather than the inner world of thoughts and feelings. The concern of the behaviourist counsellor is not to interpret the client's behaviour but to modify it.

For example, someone might be frightened of open spaces and insist on staying indoors. Someone else might become angry for no good reason and be violent in the home. The behaviourist counsellor pays no attention to the fears of the person who stays indoors and is not interested in the reasons for the anger of the violent person. What is at issue is the behaviour itself.

The attempt to change behaviour is made by a set of rewards and punishments, where a reward is anything that gives pleasure and punishment is anything that brings negative emotions. It is usually argued that the original behaviour, which is going to be changed, was established because it rewarded the individual who now continues in that pattern. The person who is frightened of open spaces might have once been caught in a thunder storm. The person who becomes angry unreasonably, it is said, does so because at some point he or she has learnt that this is a way to solve problems. But whatever established the unwanted behaviour is relatively unimportant. So long as new rewards can be brought into play, the old behaviour can be extinguished.

> the attempt to change behaviour is made by a set of rewards and punishments

The adult who is frightened of open spaces might be taught to cope with large rooms, and then enclosed outdoor areas before finally venturing into completely open spaces outdoors. Each step forward is rewarded, perhaps simply by praising the achievement. Similarly, the unreasonably angry person might be enabled to solve problems in a way that did not create more problems. Again, each step would be rewarded until a new pattern had been learnt.

Psychodynamic counselling

Here counsellors work with the ideas of Sigmund Freud (1956–1939), Carl G Jung (1875–1961) or Alfred Adler (1870–1937) or others whose work contributes to modern psychotherapy. Broadly speaking this approach is very interested in thoughts and feelings and delves into the reasons why human beings act as they do. Observed behaviour is not nearly as important here as the unconscious thoughts and feelings of the human personality. The counsellor in this tradition is interested in dreams (when thoughts and feelings roam out of control), slips of the tongue (is there some hidden reason for them?), patterns of forgetfulness (is an idea being unconsciously suppressed?) and relationships with parents and brothers and sisters in early childhood since it is thought that these lay down patterns which continue in later life.

Freud, Jung and Adler, who knew each other and initially worked together, built different models of the human personality and proposed different mechanisms to explain personal development. Freud, whose background was liberal Jewish, was the most hostile to religion and could be described as an atheist. Jung came from a family of Protestant pastors and was sympathetic to religion, though his own beliefs were far from orthodox. Adler was a humanist who did not believe in the reality of God except as an ideal.

The models of human personality these men constructed shared a belief in the unconscious mind and the ego or 'I', the sense of personal identity. In Freud's model, there is a battle between the unconscious mind, which is full of repressed childish desires, and the conscience, which has been instilled by authoritative adults. The ego mediates between the demands of these two forces. Jung believed in a collective as well as an individual unconscious and Adler's view of the unconscious was minimal, but in each case the ego is the rational decision-making part of the human being.

Freud placed enormous emphasis on the child's sexual development and explained many adult complications by reference to what he thought was happening in the child's mind. Jung disagreed with Freud's emphasis on childhood sexuality and it was on this matter that the two men parted company. As a result any counsellor who deals with the sexual abuse of children is likely to find it difficult to avoid working with some of Freud's ideas.

Counsellors who work in the psychodynamic tradition make use of what they call 'transference' when they believe that the thoughts and feelings of the client may be displaced from a parent or significant adult to the counsellor him or herself. Fear about losing a parent, for instance, might turn into fear of losing the counsellor, but the counsellor reacts calmly and rationally and so helps solve the problem.

The basic method of treatment is for the counsellor to listen to the counsellee. The counsellor might listen to a person who becomes angry irrationally and begin to explain what is happening by reference to early relationships with a parent.

> the basic method of treatment is for the counsellor to listen to the counsellee

Perhaps a male client would be told that in becoming angry with his wife, he was really directing resentment at his mother for her treatment of him as a child. Perhaps a female client would be told that her rebellion against authority figures stemmed from a desire to overthrow the influence of a strict father. By learning to understand the hidden sources of anger or resentment, the client could deal with strong feelings and improve personal relationships.

Self-theory counselling

This follows the work of Carl Rogers (1902–1987) who argued that there are natural drives within human beings leading them to 'self-actualisation' – which is a mixture between self-expression, fulfilment, happiness and self-acceptance.

According to Rogers everyone develops a self-image (an idea of what they are really like) but this may be quite different from our day-to-day behaviour and what others think we are really like. Consequently there may be a large gap between what we think of ourselves and the information fed back to us by others. This can lead to situations where other people think we are successful and we think we are failures or where we think we are successful and other people think we are failures.

The properly adjusted person, the self-actualiser, knows a match between the self-image and social reality. The neurotic person, by contrast, has lost contact with his or her own true feelings and values and has taken on the values of others.

Though Rogers changed elements of his approach during his life, his basic position was that people contain within themselves the resources for solving their problems. Rogers had grown up in a conservative Christian home and, at one stage, had begun to train for the ministry, but his free-thinking led him towards the humanistic position that lies behind his theory.

The Rogerian counsellor must, first of all, be 'transparent' or completely honest with the client but, at the same time, non-judgmental. The counsellor must offer the client 'unconditional positive regard' or caring understanding and sympathy. Counsellors must be able to feel what their client is feeling and the counselling sessions often follow a sequence where the counsellor simply reflects back to the client what he or she has said. The client says, 'I can not believe that I passed my driving test' and the counsellor says 'You feel pleased that you passed your driving test'. Counsellors use a large number of sentences starting with the words 'You feel...' to try to reflect the feelings of the client accurately and, at the same time, to build up the client's sense that his or her feelings are valuable. Given the theory that anxiety occurs when people lose contact with their own feelings, this is an understandable strategy. Given the implication that lack of self-worth can be countered by genuine regard, this is a sensible line to take.

> the counsellor must offer the client understanding and sympathy

One of the features of Rogers' approach that became well known was his 'non-directive' style. The client would *not* be told, 'This is wrong' or 'Your anger against your wife is harming you'. No direction about what the client should or should not do was given by the counsellor. By being non-directive and passing no judgement on the client, Rogers thought the client would eventually come to work out what he or she ought to do, and the client was in the best position to do this. The counsellor must, at all costs, avoid foisting his or her values on the client. The client's values are as valuable as the counsellor's.

> one of the features of Rogers' approach was his 'non-directive' style

The non-directive style adopted by Rogers became more specifically 'client-centred' and then, finally, 'person-centred' so that both client and counsellor were expected to change as a result of the counselling sessions (Hurding, 1995:750).

Differences between psychodynamic and Rogerian counselling are summarised overleaf (adapted from McLeod and Wheeler, 1996:9)

Tools and basics derived from humanistic approaches

Humanistic approaches have led to several tools that have been adapted and used in counselling. One of the best known of these is a system of measuring personality using a questionnaire called the

Psychodynamic	Person-centered
Unconscious process	Conscious process
Use of dreams	Dream work not emphasised
Therapist: no self disclosure	Therapist: may include self disclosure
Professional distance	Shows warmth
Focus on underlying anxiety	Focus on experiencing feelings
Linking past and present	Focus on past, present or future
Look for what is hidden	Accepts clients where they are
History-taking essential	The past sometimes irrelevant
Vast theoretical literature	Limited theoretical literature
Theory gender-orientated	Theory has no implications for gender
Sees people as destabilised by self-destructive instincts	Sees people as fundamentally good

Myers-Briggs Type Indicator, or MBTI for short. This indicator conceives of personality as fitting four dimensions:

- extroversion/introversion (E/I)
- intuition/sensing (N/S)
- thinking/feeling (T/F)
- judging/perceiving (J/P)

The first dimension concerns *orientation*. The extrovert is orientated towards the outer world of people and events. The introvert is orientated towards the inner world of thoughts and feelings. The extrovert enjoys the stimulation of many people, colour, loud music and the excitement of risks; the introvert enjoys the tranquillity of a few friends, soft music and a lifestyle that allows time for solitude.

The second dimension concerns *information gathering*. The intuitive person gathers information about the world by trying to grasp a situation whole, by understanding it through ideas. The sensing person gathers information through the five senses, through the details of a situation.

The third dimension concerns *decision-making*. The thinking person makes decisions on the basis of reasons, objective evidence and analysis. The feeling person makes decisions on the basis of personal feelings and subjective factors.

The fourth dimension concerns the *lifestyle*. The judging person prefers order, punctuality, planning and time keeping. The perceiving person prefers to be spontaneous, freely adjusting to new plans and vague about time, dates and calendars.

These dimensions can be put into 16 possible combinations. So, someone can be ENTJ (Extrovert, Intuitive, Thinking and Judging), for example, or INTJ (Introvert, Intuitive, Thinking and Judging) or ISTJ (Introvert, Sensing, Thinking and Judging). The advantage of the system from a counselling point of view is that all the 16 types have some good qualities. There is a positive aspect to all the types and no one type is better than the others. This enables people to accept themselves. For instance, the ENTJ fits the profile of a leader. Such a person has no difficulty in relating to others (E), thinks of possibilities in situations (N), makes rational decisions (T) and is reliable and organised (J). But the INTJ also has qualities. In this case the introvert is the original thinker, the scientist perhaps or the philosopher, some-one whose orientation to the inner world allows him or her to pursue plans and ideas over a long period of time without being distracted.

On the other hand the ISTJ may make an ideal accountant, book keeper, contract lawyer, and so on. This person is precise, careful, at home with detail, willing to spend time with documents, rational in decision-making and organised in lifestyle. The complications arise when one type is married to another or tries to operate in the realm for which they are not fitted. But the beauty of the system is that it allows people who are aware of it to respect the gifts and talents of others without forcing them to be what they are not. Further details of the system are given by Briggs-Myers and Myers (1980), Myers and McCaulley (1985), Kroeger and Thuesen (1992), Bayne (1995) and Innes (1996).

We suggest Christian uses of the MBTI later in this chapter.

Another tool useful in counselling is the Social Readjustment Rating Scale (Holmes and Rahe, 1967) that deals with levels of stress. The most stressful event was the death of a spouse (ranked 100), followed by divorce (73), marital separation (65), jail term (63), death of a close family member (63), personal injury or illness (53), marriage (50), retirement (45) and moving on down the scale through pregnancy (40), taking out a substantial mortgage (31), change to different line of work (36), sex difficulties (39), son or daughter leaving home (29), spouse begins or stops work (26), revision of personal habits (24), trouble with the boss at work (23), change in residence (20), change in church activities (19), change in eating habits (15), holiday (13), Christmas (12) and minor violation of the law (11). Unfortunately, these stress factors tend to come together so that people may marry, move house and change jobs in quick succession. Studies have shown that when people experience a score of 300 units or more, especially over a short period of time, they are more susceptible to physical illness.

Christian counsellors may wish to use the scale to work out whether stress levels are too high so they can give appropriate advice. They should notice that marriage, holidays and Christmas are, perhaps unexpectedly, stress-related events.

The basis for counselling, especially in a Rogerian setting, is sympathetic non-directedness. The counsellor, as part of professional ethics, and certainly as part of professional training, knows that there are boundaries which must not be transgressed. The counsellor reflects rather than advises, listens rather than speaks, expresses supporting feelings rather than moral judgements. This basis, which respects the personality of the counsellee, may be transferred, with modifications, into a Christian context. It is a useful counterbalance to the approach to pastoral counselling where the pastor does all the talking and the counsellee cannot get a word in edgeways, and retires depressed and frustrated.

> marriage, holidays and Christmas are, perhaps unexpectedly, stress-related events

Criticisms of humanistic approaches

The approaches are critical of each other. Behaviourists argue that the psychodynamic approaches deal with ideas that cannot be verified. Perhaps someone is resentful of a parent, but perhaps not. There is no way of knowing. All we do know is what a client's present behaviour is and there is no good reason for assuming that the events of childhood are a key to the mature adult. People with similar sorts of childhood turn out in adult life to be very different. People with different sorts of childhood turn out to be very similar. Moreover, there is some evidence that clients who attend psychodynamic counsellors may become more ill as a consequence and that others, who do not attend, become well spontaneously without any need for therapy.

From the other side, the psychodynamic approaches argue that behaviourism ignores many of the most important things about human beings, their feelings and thoughts, and that to treat unhappy humans like animals who must be trained by rewards and punishments is belittling and unsatisfactory.

Christian criticisms of these models of personality must deal with:

1. The idea of the self;
2. The idea of the unconscious;
3. The idea that people have all resources they need to solve their problems within themselves.

The self

The Christian idea of the self, derived from the bible, is both positive and negative. Christians are commanded to love their neighbours as themselves, a command that would make no sense if they did not love themselves. Likewise, husbands are commanded to look after their wives as they look after their own bodies, because no one hates his own body (Eph 5:29). On the other side, Christians are told to be prepared to deny themselves in the cause of discipleship (Mt 16:24). They are told to put off the 'old self' (Col 3:9) and that the 'old self' is crucified with Christ (Rom 6:6).

The doctrine of the resurrection of the body implies the continuation of Christian individuality in eternal life. If individuality is retained – that is, if Christians are not simply swallowed up in the glory of God in the eternal state – then something of the self remains. This self is, as is clear both from the Gospels and the Epistles (Jn 15, Col. 1:27), united with Christ.

Christianity does not, therefore, teach that the self is automatically good or that, if it is allowed freedom and the chance for expression, all will be well. On the contrary the self may be destructive of itself or of other selves. It may be immature as well as manipulative and driven by a callous will (Rom 9).

The unconscious

The idea of the unconscious is essential to psychodynamic theories. From the Christian point of view it is important to remember that the person is seen as a whole. The description of the way Christians should love God with all their mind, soul, heart and strength is matched by a description of the Christian as having a spirit, soul and body, all of which

> if there is an unconscious mind, the Christian's unconscious mind is redeemed

may be made holy (1 Thess 5:23). The whole mind can love Christ
(otherwise the command would not have been given) and the whole
person can be made holy. The point at issue is that the salvation
provided by Christ affects the *whole person,* not simply the conscious
part. If there is an unconscious mind, the Christian's unconscious mind
is redeemed. We say 'if' because the evidence for the unconscious is
fragmentary and elusive. It shows that we cannot remember everything
we know all at once, but not that we have a mind into which, like an
underground cellar, we shut away all that is undesirable about ourselves and our experiences.

Our resources

 The humanistic conception of people must, by definition, insist that
people have, within themselves, all they need to solve their problems.
Humanists think we are 'alone on the earth' and there is no God on
whom we may call for help. The Christian position is that, by surrendering to the grace of God, people are enabled to do what they could
not otherwise do. God will give grace in time of need (Heb 4:16). The
two viewpoints are opposed.

Christian ethics and counselling

The man or woman who comes to a Christian minister for help does
so with an attitude of trust and in the expectation that the Christian
minister will not exploit the counselling situation. Ministerial ethics
absolutely demand that the minister acts entirely for the good of
the counsellee. For example the Christian minister will, by virtue
of the counselling situation, become privy to embarrassing secrets. As part of the trust that is at the heart of the counselling
process, the minister must be prepared to keep these secrets and not to
indulge in gossip.

There may be situations where a minister would like to discuss a
particular difficulty with a fellow minister or with his or her spouse. If this
is so, the counsellor should make it clear to the counsellee that this is what
is likely to happen. There are, unfortunately, pitfalls in the counsellor's

path when he or she is unable to share a problem with a spouse since a greater degree of intimacy on a particular issue will be achieved between the counsellor and the counsellee than between the counsellor and his or her spouse. Such intimacy can put a strain on the counsellor's marriage.

We would contend that Christian counselling:

- guarantees confidentiality between counsellor and counsellor (but with the provision made above);
- guarantees the counsellor will act in the best interests of the counsellee;
- recognises the faith commitment of the counsellor at the outset (that is, does not expect the counsellor to act in way contrary to Christian teaching);
- recognises that, as a result of this faith commitment, the Christian counsellor will see a good outcome in the enhanced Christian faith and lifestyle of the counsellee.

Briefly, both the counsellor and counsellee should know what they expect of each other.

Christian adaptations of humanistic approaches

In two sensitive and learned books Hurding (1985; 1992) deals with the way Christians may use counselling theories and techniques originally developed in a secular framework. In a similar vein Meier, Minirth, Wichern and Ratcliff (1991), also show where areas of compatibility lie.

Historically Christians who have tried to bring pastoral care and counselling together have often assimilated their pastoral care into the secular or religious trends of their day. Leslie Weatherhead, the Methodist, wished to see collaborative work take place between medical doctors and Christian ministers and treated his own clients to a miniature version of Freudian analysis and, where he felt unable to help, passed them on to a skilled clinician. Weatherhead's own position, towards the end of his life, had only the barest traces of biblical Christianity. He wrote *The Christian Agnostic* in 1965 and dabbled in psychic phenomena. Similarly, the Westminster Pastoral Foundation (WPF), that began as an attempt to let Christian ministry operate side by side with the medical profession and social workers, has now reached a position where 'at no time is counselling an attempt to convert a client or to unduly influence a client to any particular creed or philosophy of life' and the 1982 Short Course Programme included seminars that used the signs of the Zodiac and Tarot cards as a 'map for the journey' (Hurding, 1985:226). The liberal Christian position, in other words, tends to lose sight of its origins and to be swallowed up by humanistic theories or New Ageism.

Nevertheless there are Christian versions of secular positions. The numerous books of James Dobson have a behaviouristic flavour. In *Dare to Discipline* (1970) the parent is taught how to reward and punish the child to obtain the desired behaviour. In the work of Selwyn Hughes there is an even stronger willingness to 'spoil the Egyptians' by using the insights of secular psychology without surrendering an evangelical position on the work of Christ. The needs for security, self-worth and significance are all fulfilled by a relationship with Christ. Counselling takes place by working through a 'layer' model of human personality exploring inwards from the layer of the body itself through the layers of emotion, will, and reason to the spiritual core. The counsellor assesses each layer for problems. If the body needs attention, a medical appointment is advised; if the emotions are negative, they are brought into the open and treated by using Scripture for meditation; if the will is misdirected, aims and choices are examined; if reasoning is based on false assumptions it, too, is treated by Scripture, as is the spiritual core (Hughes, 1982a; 1982b).

As part of his counselling programme, Hughes offers training to whole churches through his *Learning to Care* video course and this is in addition to the *Every Day With Jesus* bible study notes which encourage healthy and fruitful Christian living through prayer, meditation on Scripture and devotion to Christ. For those who want to pursue counselling issues more thoroughly the quarterly magazine, *Carer and Counsellor*, provides information and advice on a range of topics from a discussion on a biblical framework for counselling to practical help for those plagued by obsessive guilt.

Meier, Minirth, Wichern and Ratcliff (1991:313f) argue that 'in spite of a basic unity derived from their oneness in Christ and their acceptance of the bible as an absolute standard, Christian counsellors differ in personality, the training they have received, their experience, the setting in which they practice, and the kinds of counsellees who come to them for help'. Yet, they argue Christian counsellors have three things in common:

- they listen to the counsellee;
- they help the counsellee gain insight;
- they help the counsellee formulate a plan of action.

Listening

This is a simple and effective way of showing concern. The warmth and empathy emphasised in the person-centred approach is entirely appropriate. The counsellee must feel that the counsellor is not bored, waiting to go home, or, worse, furious with what is being said. It is helpful to remember the words of Jesus, 'I did not come to judge the world, but to save it' (Jn 12:47). The counsellor does not listen to judge, but to save.

The Christian counsellor may well believe that it is right to begin a session with prayer and to ask Christ to be present because two people, the counsellor and the counsellee, are gathered in his name. The Christian counsellor will want to be aware of the prompting and guidance of the Holy Spirit while listening. Perhaps there is a point in the counsellee's account when something is being glossed over? Perhaps these tears indicate where the real pain is? Or perhaps they don't? The words describing Jesus in Isaiah 11:2 and 3 are fitting, 'The Spirit of the Lord will rest on him – the Spirit of wisdom and understanding, the Spirit of counsel and of power, the Spirit of knowledge and fear of the Lord – and he will delight in the fear of the Lord. *He will not judge by what he sees with his eyes or decide by what he hears with his ears...*' The processes of judgement are inward, spiritual and free from hearsay and superficiality.

> the Christian counsellor will want to be aware of the prompting and guidance of the Holy Spirit while listening

Helping to gain insight

This is best done by clarifying the relationship between past and present. The Christian counsellor can bring to bear the truths of the bible to a counsellee haunted by the past. The death of Jesus on the cross secures complete and utter forgiveness of sin. The bible is emphatic about this. Sins which are scarlet may be white as snow. Iniquities (which are vile sins) are forgiven and transgression (which is wilful and deliberate sin) is removed as far as the east is from the west (i.e. the largest possible distance on an earthly scale) (Isa 1:18; Rom 4:7; Ps 103:12).

Forgiveness is offered on the basis of confession and faith (1 Jn 1:9). There are people who think their sin is worse than anyone else's and cannot be forgiven and others, at the opposite extreme, who believe that what they have done wrong is not really sinful. The counsellor can help the counsellee escape both errors.

The past is not where we live, and the counsellor can enable the counsellee to face the present and the future. The present may be complicated by destructive feelings or cycles of behaviour and the counsellor can allow the counsellee to air feelings. Often, following one of the insights of secular psychology, it may be found that anger which has been internalised and directed against oneself is the cause of depression.[9] The counsellor can also face the issues relating to destructive or dishonest behaviour. When behaviour is changed, feelings are likely to follow soon afterwards.

Meier, Minirth, Wichern and Ratcliff (1991:316) recommend an 'indirect-directive' approach, allowing the counsellee to reach conclusions about the will of God in a particular situation for him or herself, though also willing to give advice and clarification when asked to do so. If the counsellor is too directive, however, the counsellee either may not be able to carry out the directions or become completely dependent on the counsellor when new problems crop up. The intention of counselling is always to produce mature Christians who are able, within the fellowship of a congregation, to run their own lives and to respond to God individually. One useful way of helping counsellees gain insight is by asking questions that lead them to reach appropriate conclusions.

These questions may be in the form of a questionnaire, either individually or collectively. The Myers-Briggs Type Indicator (MBTI) is often helpfully introduced to people during weekend courses. It is interesting to see 20 people divided into extroverts and introverts and then the two groups asked to work separately to devise a carol service. The extroverts will probably want drama, noise, an opportunity to

---

[9.] Rational Emotive Behavior Therapy is a rough secular equivalent of the kind of analysis carried out here. See Gordon, J. and Dryden, W. (1996) 'Rational Emotive Behaviour Therapy', in S. Palmer, S. Dainow and P. Milner (eds), *Counselling: the BAC Counselling Reader*, London: Sage Publications.

meet other people during the service, and plenty of social interaction afterwards. The introverts will want good singing, little or no social interaction and a well planned sequence of readings and carols. The extroverts will enjoy preaching with plenty of jokes, asides, attempts to stir up the congregation and occasional volume. The introvert will prefer systematic exposition without frills. The extroverts will find the introvert service dull; the introverts will find the extrovert service badly thought out or too noisy. Once the differences between extroverts and introverts are understood then it is much easier in church life to prevent the kinds of irritations and clashes that take place when introverts and extroverts insist on their own preferences. When the numbers of extroverts and introverts are compared with males and females we find that males are more inclined to be extroverts and females introverts – which may explain some of the friction that occurs between the sexes! As one of the authors can testify, when an EN (extrovert, intuitive) husband is asked by his IS (introvert, sensing) wife to remember the colour of the curtains, he has no idea whether the room has any curtains!

Formulating a plan of action

This is the final stage. The problem has been analysed, the past has been faced up to, forgiven, left behind and the feelings of the present have been brought within the 'bond of peace' (Eph 4:3). A new plan should be made creatively and seriously. Alternatives should be considered in the light of Scripture and what has been learnt. The plan needs to be specific rather than general so that it is attainable and the period of time during which the first phase of the plan is to be carried out must be set in advance.

The counsellor helps to form the plan, but does not prescribe it. The plan must come from the counsellee on the basis of his or her own meditation on Scripture and prayer. This is a matter of discovering the will of God: the guidance of Scripture, of the Spirit, and of circumstances must concur.

> the counsellor helps to form the plan, but does not prescribe it

The theology of guidance corresponds with the kind of God the bible reveals. The God of the bible is ordered, personal, loving, communicative, covenant-keeping and reasonable. To put this another way, guidance is not a matter of the occasional verse of Scripture which suddenly comes to mind nor of an unsettling coincidence that has to be decoded like a secret message.

Scripture itself contains examples and principles for the Christian to follow. So, for instance, the Christian, without further ado, knows that it is wrong to steal. In trying to formulate a plan, the counsellee is looking for principles. Is marriage commended in the bible? (yes); is hard work commended in the bible? (yes); is forgiveness commended in the bible? (yes), and so on. In making this plan it is important to distinguish between the Old Testament and the New and between what has happened once and what happens often. The Christian who, on the basis of Ezekiel's visions, considers that he must prophesy to a graveyard, is likely to be mistaken. The Christian who, on the basis of Gideon's placing of a fleece on the ground to discover whether he should attack the Midianites (Judg 6), thinks this is a common method of guidance should consider whether this message was ever used anywhere else in the bible and whether it was used by the early church. The answer to these questions is negative. Scripture itself commends the advice of godly people and the wisdom they may bring from experience (Jas 3:13). It also shows how the Holy Spirit works in the life of the Christian. There is to be a perpetual guidance. Christians are to be 'led by the Spirit' (Gal 5:18) and to 'keep in step with the Spirit' (Gal 5:25). They are to know the inward prompting of the Spirit, as for instance Peter did in Acts 10:19. They may also expect the Spirit to be shown in the Christian worship through preaching or the charismatic gifts. When the inward prompting and the outward experience match, the Christian may move forward confidently. In Acts 13, Paul and Barnabas are guided, almost certainly by prophecy 'for the work to which I have called them'. The point is that the prophecy confirmed what the Lord had already told them on another, private occasion.

Finally circumstances are also a guiding. The bible shows God as being in charge of circumstances, perhaps most graphically in Jeremiah 18 where the potter (who is God) moulds a clay pot (who is the individual). In ancient times the potter caused his wheel to revolve by kicking an extension of its axle. Thus the hands of the potter shape the pot, but the feet of the potter rotate the turntable. The feet are unseen, but they govern the pot's situation.

Jay Adams' approach to counselling

Adams has vigorously rejected modern counselling methods and Freudian theories and constructed his approach entirely on the bible. He advocates 'nouthetic' counselling based on the Greek term for warning, exhortation and admonition. Adams presented his approach in the books *Competent to Counsel* (1970) and *Pastoral Counselling* (1975) and in shorter articles.

The approach consists of a series of organised and regular sessions between the minister and the person who needs help. The minister, having diagnosed the problem, in person-to-person verbal confrontation attempts to bring about change in the behaviour and attitudes of the counsellee. The textbook to be used in the verbal confrontation is the bible itself. So the approach is authoritative, directive and disciplining. The sessions follow a pattern of *dehabituation* where the old, bad habits are addressed in counselling sessions and where the counsellee 'does homework' by actively trying to throw these habits aside during daily life and *rehabituation* where the counsellee actively tries to form new habits. Adams considers that dehabituation and rehabituation happen together and, as bad habits die out, good habits replace them. The whole process can take about 12 weeks. In his experience changes only begin at the point of the counsellee's repentance so that there might be three or four weeks where no change took place, a week of crisis when repentance occurred and then a further six or eight weeks when the old habits were replaced by the new ones (Adams, 1975:21).

The approach is mental (or cognitive) and behavioural. It is directed towards the mind and behaviour rather than to emotions. And the methods to promote dehabituation and rehabituation may use rewards and punishments, but not crudely and, in a development of the theory, Adams is careful to ensure that Christians who are being counselled in this way are helped by other members of a congregation. A woman who is depressed and unable to do anything at home might be paired with another woman who is able to encourage and help practically (Adams, 1975:33). Where counselling

where counselling sessions appear to have failed, the counsellor should evaluate what has taken place sessions appear to have failed, the counsellor should evaluate what has taken place and be prepared to admit failure to the counsellee, and, if the counselling has concerned a married couple, to the counsellees (Adams, 1975:57).

As you will have guessed Adams's approach is controversial because it runs against the prevalent Rogerian and Freudian currents and it is thought by Meier *et al.* (1991:274) to be unwise in attributing all stresses and emotional problems to personal sins and irresponsibility and by Hurding (1985:286) to deny the existence of mental illness and to be based on a limited view of human nature.

Nevertheless Adams is a valuable force against the tendency to throw the riches of Christian theology away in favour of counselling theories that have their roots in non- or anti-Christian positions.

In the chapters that follow, we acknowledge the strength of Adams's position while feeling free to call on the insights of other methods.[10]

References

Adams, J.E. (1970), *Competent to Counsel,* Nutley: Presbyterian and Reformed Publishing Company.

Adams, J.E. (1975), *Pastoral Counselling*, Grand Rapids: Baker Book House.

Bayne, R. (1995), *The Myers-Briggs Type Indicator: a Critical Review and Practical Guide*, London: Chapman and Hall.

Briggs-Myers, I. and Myers, I.B. (1980), *Gifts Differing*, Palo Alto, California: Consulting Psychologists Press.

Dobson, J. (1970), *Dare to Discipline,* Eastbourne: Kingsway Publication.

Holmes, T.H. and Rahe, R.T. (1967), The Social Readjustment Rating Scale, *in Journal of Psychosomatic Research*, II, 213–218.

Hughes, S. (1982a), *A Friend in Need*, Eastbourne: Kingsway Publications.

Hughes, S. (1982b), *The Christian Counsellor's Pocket Guide,* Eastbourne: Kingsway Publications.

Hurding, R.F. (1985), *Roots and Shoots: a Guide to Counselling and Psychotherapy*, London: Hodder and Stoughton.

Hurding, R .F. (1992), *The Bible and Counselling*, London: Hodder and Stoughton.

[10.] Lynch, G. (1996) Where is the theology of British pastoral counselling? in *Contact* 121, 22-28, points out that the theological critique of pastoral counselling has been remarkably limited, almost non-existent.

Hurding, R.F. (1995), Carl Rogers, in *New Dictionary of Christian Ethics and Pastoral Theology,* D.J. Atkinson, D.H. Field, O. O'Donovan and A.F. Holmes (eds), Leicester: Inter-Varsity Press.

Innes, R. (1996), *Personality Indicators and the Spiritual Life*, Cambridge: Grove Books Ltd.

Kroeger, O. and Thuesen, J.M. (1992), *Type Talk at Work*, New York: Delacorte Press.

McLeod, J. and Wheeler, S. (1996), Person-centred and psychodynamic counselling: a dialogue, in *Counselling: the BAC Counselling Reader* S. Palmer, S. Dainow and P. Milner, (eds), London: Sage Publications.

Meier, P.D., Minirth, F.B., Wichern F.B.and Ratcliff, D.E. (1991), *Introduction to Psychology and Counselling* (2nd edition), Tunbridge Wells: Monarch.

Myers, I.B. and McCaulley, M.H. (1985), *Manual: a Guide to the Development and Use of the Myers-Briggs Type Indicator*, Palo Alto.

Palmer, S., Dainow, S. and Milner, P. (1996), *Counselling: the BAC Counselling Reader*, London: Sage Publications.

"You can always tell a good Counsellor by their ears!"

Chapter 12

COUNSELLING: WHEN, WHERE AND HOW

Bible Basis   *2 Timothy 2:21-24*

Duration, privacy and morality

Counselling may be given in the course of pastoral ministry. The pastor may counsel a member of the congregation after a Sunday service or during a routine programme of home visits. This sort of counselling often requires only one meeting and is given on the basis of a crisis or problem that has suddenly occurred. The counsellee often asks for a meeting with the minister rather than the other way round.

More long-term counselling is needed for more long-term problems. In these instances, the minister may suggest meeting, but should not insist on it: counselling, if it is to be successful, is a voluntary activity and should be offered, not required.

All counselling needs privacy and time. Privacy is secured by a quiet room free from a telephone. Time is secured by an appointment system. The danger of privacy is that immorality may either take place or be thought to have taken place. The only safeguard in these circumstances is to ensure that one-to-one counselling is avoided. The minister's spouse is often helpfully present if the minister needs to counsel a member of the opposite sex. Unmarried ministers must make other arrangements, often by asking another church member to sit in on the counselling session or counselling in the presence of the spouse of the person who has the long-term problem.

Place and time

The general approach to counselling should be friendly but business-like. A cup of tea or coffee can make the counselling session more like an ordinary social occasion and this feeling is reinforced if everyone sits in a rough circle in an easy chair. The slight formality produced by notetaking does no harm, and it may be unavoidable

> the general approach to counselling should be friendly but business-like

if the minister is to recall all the details of every counselling encounter. In a small congregation it is often convenient to meet in the evening in the minister's home or, alternatively, where church facilities allow this, in a private room on church premises.

An hour is usually sufficient for a counselling session. The advantage of a regular weekly session is that the counsellee has a fixed point in the week where problems can be shared and progress reviewed. And 'progress' is the word that must be emphasised. The implication for a pastoral ministry that puts counselling at its centre is that half a dozen members of a congregation can monopolise ministerial time either to the detriment of other activities or to the displeasure of less demanding members of the congregation. The minister must therefore be able to show that counselling solves problems and is not simply a permanent feature of his or her lifestyle (failing with large groups, he or she is happiest with one person at a time) or of the counsellee's lifestyle (being lonely, he or she finds the friendliness of the minister a substitute for other relationships).

Purpose

Clearly, if counsellees are not making progress, none will be discharged and the minister will add more and more to his or her case load until the week is completely filled with counselling appointments to the exclusion of all else. When this happens, the minister's public duties are performed badly and the congregation as a whole suffers.

Ideally, counselling is a pastoral activity that *complements other pastoral activities*. The minister's preaching is itself a powerful tool in the healing process the counsellee is seeking. What is said from the pulpit should underline what is said privately and enable the counsellee to begin to fit into ordinary congregational activity. This is the best outcome. If the counsellee resists attendance at church services, the minister will suspect that he or she is being used to fill a gap in the counsellee's life and that the counsellee does not really want to serve God. Indeed, the counsellee may be surprisingly manipulative. 'You must come and see me tomorrow. I have got something very important to tell you' or 'Thank you for helping me solve my problem. But I think you have shown me that I have another one I need help with.' Since the minister does not charge an hourly fee for counselling, such requests are viewed with suspicion.

The problem

The minister's initial aim is to find out the nature of the counsellee's problem. This may not be as straightforward as it appears at first sight. The counsellee may 'present' with one problem ('I am worried about my husband') but actually be aware of another ('my sexual relationship with my husband is unhappy'). Diagnosis may be made by setting the events that led up to the problem in chronological order. The counsellee, because of worry and confusion, may have difficulty in placing events in a coherent sequence and of seeing how the same events may look from the viewpoints of the different people involved in them.

The process of putting events in order and working out how different participants perceive the situation will often enable counsellees to gain a clarity that has previously eluded them. In this sense, a Rogerian non-directive approach (see previous chapter) is a useful beginning.

Ministers whose theological viewpoint lays stress on spiritual forces may be inclined to diagnose a counsellee's problems by reference to demons. 'You have a demon of gluttony and it needs to be cast out.' Such snap diagnoses are unchallengeable because they are thought to stem from charismatic discernment (1 Cor 12).

a Rogerian non-directive approach (see previous chapter) is a useful beginning

The trouble with these diagnoses is that, if they are wrong, they do immense damage to the counsellee.[11]

What may happen is that the minister attempts to cast the demon out and the counsellee must then react. If the counsellee refuses to

[11] The discernment of 1 Corinthians 12:10 must be matched against the collective judgemant that takes place in 1 Corinthians 14:29–32 with regard to prophecy. Since the most powerful of the verbal *charismata* is subject to judgement, it is reasonable to suppose the other *charismata* should meet a similar requirement.

react, the demon is in control and is rebelling against divine authority. When the counsellee reacts (by sighing or falling over, or whatever), the demon is said to have been cast out. A little later, the counsellee may find the problem has not been solved and the gluttony (in this instance) returns. If this is admitted to the minister, he or she probably goes to the text which speaks of the demon finding seven other demons and reinhabiting a spring cleaned house (Mt 12:45). So, there are now seven demons to cast out. In any case the minister goes through the exorcism procedure again, and the cycle continues, sometimes several times. In short, an incorrect diagnosis, once made, cannot be seen to be wrong, and the counsellee is allowed to take the blame for letting the situation deteriorate after the 'first demon' has been cast out.

An alternative reading of the situation would suggest that there was no demon of gluttony present in the first place. The misdiagnosis has led to a repetition of the problem. Had the problem been correctly diagnosed and treated, it would not have recurred.

The Christian minister is on much safer theological ground in emphasising the reality of the new birth, the operation of the Holy Spirit in enabling the individual to overcome sin and the power of persistent prayer.

And now...

In the chapters that follow, we outline a problem, its possible causes and the areas counselling might try to resolve. The problems are given in alphabetical order.

We have not assumed that all the people whom the counsellor meets will be Christian, but we believe that the problems of the non-Christian are largely solved by accepting Christ and we make no apology for the occasional intrusion of this assumption.

We have sometimes referred to the minister in the sections that follow, sometimes to the counsellor and sometimes to the minister/counsellor to indicate that the roles are hard to disentangle and overlapping. We wish to emphasise that the Christian counsellor will feel free to offer prayer and to share from Scripture, and in this respect is quite distinct from a secular counsellor, even though both may wish to help their counsellees equally sincerely.

Many counselling dilemmas have a moral dimension and minster/counsellors will receive help not only from counselling perspectives but also by studying Christian ethics. Norman L. Geisler's *Christian Ethics: options and issues* (Leicester: Apollos, 1989) and David Cook's *Living in the Kingdom: the ethics of Jesus* (London: Hodder and Stoughton, 1992) are both helpful. A general and well informed introduction to social and personal ethics is given in John Stott's *Issues Facing Christians Today* (London: Marshall Pickering, 1990). A more advanced text that deals with specifically medical ethics is edited by J.F. Kilner, Nigel M. de S. Cameron and David L. Shiedermayer *Bioethics and the Future of Medicine: a Christian appraisal* (Carlisle: Paternoster Press, 1995). Kilner *et al.* deal with abortion and euthanasia in considerable detail as well as general issues concerning values and medicine.

Weep with those who weep

Chapter 13

BEREAVEMENT

Bible Basis   *Acts 7:57–8:2*
                   John 17

What the Christian counsellor should expect

When someone dies, it is the survivors who suffer. People speak of having 'lost' a friend, a brother, a mother, a father, a spouse. A sense of irreplaceable absence grips the human heart.

The bereaved person very frequently is unable to come to terms with the loss. This is the state of *shock*. He or she feels that the person who has died will return, that they have simply gone away for a while and one day will walk in through the door.

After this initial sense of loss and bewilderment the next stage that often follows in the process of bereavement is *anger*. Why should this particular person whom I care about have died? If the bereaved person is a Christian there may be a temptation to *blame* God for the loss. There may also be a temptation to blame oneself. The mother whose child has been killed running across the road may continually blame herself for letting the child go out to play. The wife whose husband has died of a heart attack, may blame herself for not having seen the warning signs earlier. It is very common for the bereaved person to show remorse and think '*If only I had done*... then my brother, husband, wife, son would be alive.'

After the sense of bewilderment and loss and anger comes a more mature reflection on what has occurred.

For friends and for ministers the question arises about what should be done for the bereaved person. The one piece of advice that can be given is that the bereaved person is likely to want to talk about the whole experience. The minister may feel there is nothing to be said apart from assuring the bereaved he or she is not to blame. And so there is a tendency for the minister, and not just the minister, to avoid the bereaved person. In fact bereaved people often feel social outcasts because they know that whenever they walk into a room or meet friends they are going to cast a shadow over the conversation.

The minister must, for these reasons, allow bereaved people to talk about themselves, the situation in which the person who has died was last seen, the days and hours prior to the death and the feelings and plans of the bereaved. Bereavement is not social leprosy; it is something that happens to us all. So the minister must 'weep' with those who weep (Rom 12:15). He or she must be prepared to empathise with the bereaved, either by listening or simply by sitting in silence.

One of the authors can remember visiting a hospital where his mother had died. In a small room set aside for the purpose the attending doctor instinctively reached out a hand. The human contact, the sense that other people care is reassuring.

Some Christians take the mistaken view that it is wrong to feel sadness on the occasion of someone else's death. They say 'John has gone to heaven. Why should we grieve?' But that is to misunderstand the situation. John may have gone to heaven but we on earth feel the loss.

Moreover, there is biblical precedent for mourning. When Stephen was martyred devout men 'made great lamentation over him' (Acts 8:2). The early church wept to see one of the bright young Christians of their day stoned to death. So, if the early church with their burning conviction of heaven and of eternal life, were willing to mourn, then we should not be ashamed to do so either.

> if we cannot weep, then we cannot laugh

Indeed, psychologically mourning is a helpful process. If we repress emotions and pretend that we feel no sense of loss, then we repress *all our emotions*. The reduction of one emotion blocks out other emotions. If we cannot weep, then we cannot laugh. The long-term stunting of the emotions follows.

The Funeral

The minister has a particular role to play during the funeral. It is helpful to talk about the practical events with the bereaved person or the bereaved family and not simply to leave this to the undertaker. The minister has an opportunity to speak to the family and to say something that will be remembered. It is usual on these occasions to ask for some kind of tribute or memorial to be spoken about the person who has died. And here it is helpful to have a tribute from either the minister him or herself or from old friends. The tribute(s) should be brief and should concentrate on the characteristics of the person who has died which everyone remembers and appreciates.

Families differ in their ability to cope with bereavement and in their ability to organise funeral arrangements. Experience of funerals may give the minister an advisory role here. The whole service is divided into two main sections: first at the church and second at the grave side.

At the church the minister has little opportunity to counsel. The funeral address should be dignified and sincere. *A Manual for Ministers* (Lifestream Publications, 1993) gives details of the conduct of the service.

At the graveside (or committal) only close family and friends will be present. The minister may need to be supportive of those whose feelings overcome them at the sight of the coffin in the ground. But often family members will comfort each other and the minister is advised to let the set Scripture readings of committal speak for themselves.

The funeral service is a formal and public expression of both loss and hope. Bereaved people may appear to be 'taking it well' in the period between the death and the funeral. Only at the funeral itself may their emotions overwhelm them. Thereafter the feelings of bewilderment, pain and self-condemnation can continue to come and go sporadically. The minister/counsellor may have to offer most help in the months that follow.

The work of the minister/counsellor is to enable the bereaved to build their lives again and to face the future.

Anniversaries

One of the least understood problems that people have in facing bereavement is that the sense of loss continues well beyond the first few days and months. Whenever anniversaries occur, for example, when it is Christmas or the birthday of people who have died, it is natural to remember them. So the process of adjusting to loss is prolonged.

The minister must be sensitive. Some families will be helped by knowing what to expect. Others will feel bereavement is endless if they think ahead. In either event the minister should be prepared to let people talk about how they feel well beyond the first few months and to listen sympathetically.

Children

The most difficult bereavements to cope with are those concerning children. Here a life has hardly begun before it is over. There is very little to look back on and very little comfort to be drawn from the life that has been lived. Again, the minister is in a very difficult position. There is nothing that can be said to take away the pain, and even the most profound theological truths can sound like empty words in the face of inexplicable loss.

Even so, the minister must, as far as possible, offer practical help, availability, and be prepared to speak to those who have been bereaved.

Although there are parents who become fixed in time and who turn the dead child's bedroom into a kind of museum, there are others who turn their bereavement into something positive. They use the occasion of a death of a child to campaign for road safety or against drugs or whatever circumstances led to the child's death. The Dunblane parents have converted their grief into a campaign against the holding of guns. This is a way of making something positive out of the loss of their children, and is a very good thing to do. It gives a sense of purpose to those who have been bereaved and allows them to feel that the children who died did not live in vain.

Further reading

Among the most helpful books on this difficult subject are:

Lewis, C.S. (1966), *A Grief Observed*, London: Faber.
Vanauken, S. (1989), *Severe Mercy*, London: Hodder.

Additional information on the conduct of funerals can be found in Appendix 2.

Chapter 14

DEPRESSION, FAMILY PROBLEMS AND LOW SELF-ESTEEM

Depression

Bible Basis   *Psalm 34*
                   Psalm 42

It is very difficult for those who do not feel depression to understand those who are immersed in it. The undepressed person may be tempted to tell the depressed person to 'pull yourself together' or to 'snap out of it' or to go and do something simple and practical that will 'take your mind off your self'.

Yet depression is something altogether more deep-seated than a flattening of the emotions or a sense of deep sadness. It appears to grip the will and the ability to think. Consequently, depression affects not only feelings but also behaviour. People exhibit many varing symptoms. They may sleep less or irregularly, lose concentration, find no pleasure in personal relationships or their normal treats, do not feel like eating, or, alternatively eat far too much in a form of 'comfort' eating. They may become listless and, underneath, feel a sense of worthlessness. Manic depression alternates periods of misery with intense elation so that the manic is either 'up' or 'down' but never on a level.

Counselling and cure

Some depression is triggered by external events. Perhaps a relationship breaks down or disappointment occurs and this leads to sadness which then results in depression. Such kinds of depression are more easily dealt with since they arise from the individual's circumstances rather than from something within the individual. The more difficult kind of depression occurs when something within the individual appears to trigger it off (Dominian, 1976).

The job of the counsellor is to try to discover what has led to the depression and then to enable the depressed person to put this right. The difficulty is that the depressed person often feels unable to take any steps against the source of depression. Depressed Christians may find prayer or bible reading impossible and may not wish to attend worship since they are ashamed or guilty about their state of mind. In this way the depression is continued because the depressed person is cut off from the cures that might be offered. The same kind of pattern occurs in the case of those who become overweight, become depressed about their overweight, and then eat to comfort themselves because they are depressed. This leads to further depression and so the cycle continues endlessly. A similar pattern may occur in forms of alcoholism or in the taking of drugs, even prescribed ones, where indulgence leads via a bout of drunken or drugged forgetfulness to the cold light of day, and a desire to escape into forgetfulness once again.

The counsellor can provide friendship and warmth for the depressed person and can help formulate a new plan for living. If the depression is obviously caused by circumstances, then the counsellor/minister can help the depressed person to look at the situation differently. There may be a lesson to be learnt from the 'trial' and a purification of personal faith brought about by the heat of the opposition (1 Pet 4:12; Lloyd-Jones, 1964). The situation may indirectly bring benefit to others – Paul speaks of comforting the Corinthian congregation with the comfort he has received from God (1 Cor 1:4). The pain may be like corporal punishment that is unpleasant at the time but, afterwards, produces a 'harvest of righteousness and peace' (Heb 12:11).

From a non-theological perspective, it is also possible for the counsellor to help the depressed person see his or her situation differently. Goleman (1996:240) points out that teenagers who become depressed have a tendency to interpret setbacks in a depression-producing way. Life's small defeats become a reason for plunging into gloom rather than a challenge to accept and a battle to win. Research evidence suggests that training sessions can help young people to learn to face disappointments constructively, and so avoid depression in adulthood.

If the depression is less easy to unravel, the counsellor/minister can look for an underlying anger which, instead of being directed against people whose position seems to put them out of the reach of blame, is self-directed. The young woman who is angry with her father may, instead of admitting this, be tough on herself and so fall into depression. In this instance the remedy must be to forgive the father, and the counsellor will find out how accurate the diagnosis is when such a course of action is suggested. If it is vehemently refused, then it is likely to be the right thing to do.

If the causes of depression are more generalised the counsellor/minister can remind the depressed person that God gives 'a garment of praise instead of a spirit of despair' (Isa 61:3); that the bible speaks of a God who has turned our 'wailing into dancing' (Ps 30:11); that the bible contains examples of people who have been through 'the valley of the shadow of death' and come out the other side. So there are both within the psalms and within the lives of biblical characters examples of people who fought their way out of depression. In Psalm 42:5 the speaker asks, 'Why are you downcast, O my soul? Why so disturbed within me?' and then immediately says, 'Put your hope in God, for I will yet praise him, my Saviour and my God.' In other words the depressed person copes with depression by speaking to him or herself. Self-exhortation is not as silly as it sounds. Half the

> Why are you downcast, O my soul? Why so disturbed within me?

tennis professionals in the world speak to themselves when they reach a crucial stage of a match. Yet for the Christian, the earlier verses in Isaiah 61 are personally significant because this is the passage Jesus quoted at the outset of his ministry (Lk 4:16–21). Jesus announced that he came to provide an antidote to despair, and the Christian, because of his or her relationship with Christ, may draw on divine joy: 'I have told you this' said Jesus 'so that *my* joy may be *in you*' (Jn 15:11).

Ideally the depressed person will learn to transcend depression. Mel Carothers wrote a book entitled *Power in Praise* in which he outlined his work as a prison chaplain. Many of the prisoners had become depressed as a result of their imprisonment. He was able to encourage them to begin to praise God for even the little things in their prison lives for which they might be grateful and he saw several transformations take place in the lives of his flock.

This is the ideal route out of depression but not everyone can take it easily and some find that they must simply sit and wait for the depression to go. But those who are impatient with this prescription are much happier trying to fight against the depression that attacks them and, for this reason, are often able to shake depression off much more rapidly than those who simply wait for it to go away.

Family Problems

   Bible Basis   Ephesians 5:22-6:3

Family problems come in all shapes and sizes and usually conceal personal problems – a mother may be depressed, a father may be unemployed. The family nature of the problem usually arises in the relationship between parents and children. For this reason counselling will often need to be carried out collectively, with all the relevant members of the family present. The personal problems of individuals within the family may be solved, or at any rate alleviated, by addressing the family as a whole.

We consider three common scenarios:

1. the children are out of control and the parents belatedly want help;
2. the children are suffering depression or eating disorders;
3. elderly parents are asking for help from their children.

Uncontrollable children

Such children are easier to treat the younger they are. We assume that the children considered here are of school age.

We suggest that parents:

- need to agree together (and with teenage children) rules that must be kept; they need to agree what sanctions will be used if the rules are broken and should ensure that these sanctions are graduated according to the severity of the misbehaviour;
- must learn to be consistent in their enforcement of sanctions and rules; without consistency children will remain as bad as before;
- must support each other in maintaining rules;
- need to learn to remain calm and to explain to children why sanctions are being enforced: 'You must stay in because you have broken a window'. If parents fail in this, children will have little idea about why they should behave in one way rather than another.

Children usually become uncontrollable because:

- they are unintentionally rewarded for doing wrong (parents pay children particular attention after rule-breaking) and so they repeat the behaviour;
- they have not learnt the social skills to share with other children or to take turns with toys;
- they need medical attention (diabetes, deafness, for instance);
- one parent is continually supportive whatever they do and the other continually displeased whatever they do;
- they are neglected and follow the dictates of a gang or youth culture;
- they have not learnt to persist in solving a puzzle, and therefore their intellectual progress is dismal.

Depression and eating disorders among children

These are triggered by distress in the home. Children's depression is usually caused by painful relationships or events. Perhaps the child feels unable to please the parents. Perhaps the child feels the parents are too restrictive. Eating disorders may be caused by over sensitivity to the demands of beauty culture; by the way anorexia (serious under-eating) can reverse the effects of puberty (girls may stop their menstrual cycle) and look younger than they are and so allow them to dodge out of relationships with the opposite sex; by the tendency for family friction to appear at the meal table, and so for anorexics to try to avoid the occasion.

Over-eating is a learned behaviour, and there is a correlation between the obesity of parents and their children. Obesity occurs when, over a long period of time, food consumed exceeds a person's energy requirements. Over-eating may occur because food is identified as a comfort-giver. The parent, for example, who gives a crying child a sweet is setting up an association between food and consolation. This association may accelerate out of control in later life: the over-eating person becomes over-weight and experiences difficulties in health and relationships. To console him or herself in these difficulties, the over-weight person sits down to a slap-up meal! Exercise and a change in diet are the obvious remedies.

We suggest the following points should be considered:
- parents and children may need to be seen by a counsellor separately and together;
- medical help is usually needed for eating disorders;
- eating disorders point towards other problems.

Elderly parents

One or both parents may become demanding, feel aggressive or sorry for themselves, become forgetful, senile or incontinent and still wish to live with their sons or daughters.

- If there are, in the wider body of the church, people (for example retired missionaries) who are willing, for payment, to give the elderly care at home, then the elderly can avoid being admitted to an institution. Advertising in the Christian press is a good method of setting this arrangement up.
- The process of ageing produces a range of problems. A bereavement may leave a parent desolate and unable to cope with the practicalities of shopping and cleaning. A stroke may leave a parent physically handicapped and unable to cope with personal hygiene. On the other hand, the parent may be able to drive and cook and simply be lonely. Each of these needs calls for a different response.
- There are disadvantages in asking elderly parents to live in the family home that may be met by a 'granny flat', a bungalow close by or warden accommodation in the same town. If elderly parents do come to live in the family home, money will need to be spent on adapting bathrooms and other fittings. A stair lift may have to be installed, and new televisions and telephones bought.
- The emotional burden of looking after elderly parents must be jointly carried by the couple offering their home.

Counselling and cure

The supportive and non-directive form of counselling appropriate with individuals is less effective with a family. Instead the counsellor acts more as a mediator and facilitator in trying to persuade the family to follow a common aim. The counsellor will bear in mind that families function best when each person has a job or a role that does not conflict with others but which contributes to the good of all. While one parent fetches children from school, the other supervises football practice. While an older child looks after a younger child, a parent redecorates a bedroom.

The counsellor's strategy is to agree a family plan and monitor it. The plan may take into account some of the points mentioned above.

Low self-esteem

Bible Basis   *Ephesians 1:3-10*
1 John 3:1,2

Low self-esteem often accompanies depression. The symptoms of a person whose self-esteem is low may be that they do not feel adequately loved, are indecisive and constantly need approval. Teenagers who feel this way may become excessively cynical ('Nothing really matters') and be prepared to take enormous risks for the sake of excitement ('I only feel a hundred per cent alive when I ride my motorbike fast').

In an attempt to compensate for low self-esteem, it is common for people to speak disparagingly about others or to project a pompous or tough image to the world to try to gain respect.

The usual explanation for low self-esteem derives from the relationship with parents in the early years. Parents who say about their children publicly, 'Johnny is too stupid to understand' or 'He's a hopeless case' sow destructive seeds in the child's mind. Similar destructiveness can be induced by poor school teaching.

Counselling and cure

The counsellor is able to offer a non-judgmental warmth that will counteract many of the causes of low self-esteem. The counsellor can also try to uncover the main causes of low self-esteem in the individual's background and explain to him or her how they have operated to produce the lack of confidence the individual carries into later life. In essence, low self-esteem is a state of mind that has emotional consequences and, once the state of mind is changed, the emotions gradually follow.

The texts of Scripture and the good news of Jesus, however, offer the best remedy against low self-esteem. That Christ should die for the sinner is wonderful not least because it implies that the sinner is of infinite value. The person whose self-esteem is low, then, needs to understand and accept the offer of Christ's love.

References

Carothers, M.R. (1972), *Power in Praise*, Eastbourne: Kingway Publications.
Dominian, J. (1976), *Depression*, Harmondsworth: Penguin.

Goleman, D. (1995), *Emotional Intelligence*, London: Bloomsbury.
Lloyd-Jones, D.M. (1964), *Spiritual Depression: its Causes and Cure,* London: Marshall Pickering.

Character assaosination may be
remembered long after many acts of
Kindness are forgotten

Chapter 15

MARRIAGE DIFFICULTIES

Bible Basis   *Exodus 20:14*
              Psalm 128
              Proverbs 31:10-31
              Ephesians 5:22-33

Symptoms

Marriage difficulties may be caused or cause family problems, which we treat separately. In this section, we focus only on five problem areas:

- finance;
- lifestyle;
- roles;
- sexual activity;
- problem solving.

Finance

This is a common cause of marital disagreement. Our training in the use of money takes place early in life and remains with us into adulthood. Savers, spenders and givers each live in a different financial universe. Savers learn to delay buying until the necessary money is accumulated. They feel secure when there is money stored up for any eventuality. Spenders learn to buy without delay and try not think about distant needs. Givers (of whom there are not enough in the church) enjoy giving money away. They like to see the good they can do and take satisfaction in demonstrating their independence from the power of money and material possessions.

All three of these kinds of people may be imaginative or unimaginative (in MBTI terms, they may be S or N; see chapter 11). An unimaginative view of money sees it as a set of tokens to exchange for goods. An imaginative view of money sees it as a set of possibilities.

	Imagivative	Unimaginative
Savers	Lots of cost cutting ideas; bargain hunting; sophisticated insurance and pension plans	Money accumulated in bank account for 'rainy day'; danger of meanness
Spenders	Money spent in unusual ways or by buying objects that complement each other	Money spent on expensive-looking objects; the act of spending itself is enjoyed
Givers	Sophisticated gifts either using financial schemes (covenant giving) or by searching for appropriate objects; care taken to ensure gifts are of maximum benefit	Standard gift made to appeals

Married couples are unlikely to handle money in exactly the same way, especially at the start of a marriage. Sometimes it is the man who is the saver and the woman the spender, but this is not always so. Savers feel insecure if married to spenders.

We take the view:

1. Because possession of money or control of family finances gives a sense of security, it is important to understand the psychological forces at work here.
2. The combination between security and insecurity in the lives of a married couple can be met by opening several accounts, one for saving, one for joint use, one for individual projects, and so on. In this way, savers can save and spenders can spend up to an agreed limit.
3. If only one member of the couple is earning, the other member will not want to continually beg for money. Therefore the earning member should give a regular amount to the non-earning member, who then has some control over personal spending.

4. Couples need to be open with each other about their financial priorities and attitude to money, perhaps using the table above to work out what sort of people they are.
5. Financial irresponsibility may be solved by numeracy skills or biblical teaching on stewardship (Lk 16:12). Let the spouse who has accountancy skills be responsible for money matters – men should not feel threatened by this.

Lifestyle

Habits, routines and tasks may be organised in terms of space (tidy) and time (punctual) or disorganised in space (untidy) and time (un-punctual), or any combination of these. Married couples are bound to argue if their lifestyles clash.

Roles within a marriage

Roles may be worked out by negotiation between the husband and wife. Women who hate being indoors and doing housework may wish to escape into the world of paid employment. Men who hate gardening may escape into the world of books. If the wife feels she is being forced into a role she dislikes, or if the man feels his wife wishes him to conform to a role unsuitable for him, there will be constant friction unless and until the problem is discussed.

The biblical teaching given in Ephesians 5:22–33 does not define roles so much as attitudes. The husband who loves his wife may, for that love, take on a traditionally female role (e.g. cleaning the house), and vice versa, and each may be willing to do what they dislike for the sake of the marriage itself. The headship role of the husband enables him to be the initiator, however, and the wife to be the responder.

Sexual activity

This is fundamental to marriage. Frigidity or impotence need to be addressed, probably by enlisting medical help.

Males tend to be aroused sexually by visual stimuli and females by emotional stimuli. This means that wives may be unready for sexual intercourse unless they are relaxed and feel appreciated by their husbands. The sexual act itself is symbolic of the union between husband and wife (Gen 3:24) and not merely the gratification of a sexual appetite. Intercourse is thus an expression of the total relationship, a means of giving comfort and value to the partner and to be enjoyed without guilt. This implies that sexual intercourse is not only for the procreation of children. Childless couples are sometimes tempted to refrain from intercourse because they feel the act has proved to be pointless but, in such instances, they need to try to see intercourse less functionally.

The use of contraceptives is accepted by Protestants since there is a categorical difference between preventing conception (when sperm does not fertilise ovum) and abortion (destroying a fertilised ovum that is going to grow into another human being). Barrier methods of contraception have the benefit of interfering less with the woman's hormonal cycle and, for this reason, are often preferred.

The frequency of intercourse varies according to personality (extroverts tend to want intercourse more often) and according to age (younger couples enjoy more frequent intercourse than older ones); it usually ranges from between three times a week to once a month and may continue well beyond the age of seventy.

Christian counsellors consider sadism (pleasure in the inflicting of pain) and masochism (pleasure in the receipt of pain) have no place within a Christian marriage.

Problem solving

Within a marriage problem solving must be achieved by conversation. Research shows that women tend to want to talk about their feelings more than men and that men are less interested in the details of personal relationships than women. It also shows that marriages which survive are those where the couple try to adjust to each other's complaints. Moreover these complaints are far less destructively aired if they are made specific. 'When you did X, I felt Y and wish you would in future do Z' is far better than 'You are a thoughtless and selfish hypocrite'. The first statement allows a constructive response, the second is character assassination and may be remembered long after many acts of kindness have been forgotten.

According to Goleman (1996:140), women are more likely to criticise their husbands and to plunge into emotional encounters than men. To counteract this, men tend to stonewall, to defend themselves by stoic imperturbability, and this, paradoxically, leads women to raise the volume of their complaints. Husbands and wives, by adopting opposing strategies, fail to resolve their differences. Instead the husband needs to realise that the wife's anger is not necessarily a sign of personal attack: the wife wants the husband to *listen* to her complaints and *sympathise* with her rather than to try to side-step the issue with a neat practical solution. Conversely wives need to understand that their angry outbursts may be taken as personal attacks by husbands who are much more adept at coping with problems presented in the general context of the relationship. 'I love you very much, but do you think you could help me by...'

Counselling and cure

A couple wanting counselling to save a marriage are best counselled by a married couple. Counsellors should not allow themselves to become referees to a point scoring contest between the conflicting partners. Instead, and in addition to offering sympathy, the counsellors' strategy is to help the partners see their problems as being ones they can face together. The wife may think the husband is the problem. The counsellors need to bring the wife to see the problem as one she and her husband can solve together.

The counsellors should also be aware that, during the course of counselling sessions, changes in position relative to each other may take place. The husband of the troubled couple may swing from being aggressive towards his wife to being protective of her and aggressive towards the counsellors.

Christian counsellors will attempt to solve marriage problems within the biblical framework, and this may involve agreeing roles for husband and wife that do not necessarily conform to the politically correct opinions of today's fashions. Extreme feminism or its opposite, extreme laddishness, are fashions designed mainly for single people and are reactions to each other and to other cultural stereotypes. Marriage by definition entails new roles and a willingness to consider at least one other person. According to Scripture marriage is intended to be an *exclusive reciprocal commitment of self-giving love which finds its natural expression in sexual union that is likely to issue in the birth of children who will be brought up in the framework of their parents' mutual love.*

As divorce and cohabitation become more commonplace in society, Christian marriage will become more exceptional. But Christians are convinced that it is the best way to live.

References

Goleman, D. (1996), *Emotional Intelligence*, London: Bloomsbury.

Additional information on the conduct of weddings can be found in Appendix 1.

Chapter 16

SEXUAL ORIENTATION

Bible Basis   *1 Corinthians 6:9–11*

Discussion of homosexuality distinguishes between the *orientation* of attraction between people of the same sex and *behaviour* where this attraction leads to sexual intimacy. Homosexuality is the generic term that includes males and females; lesbianism refers to female homosexuality.

The most reliable and recent survey of sexual behaviour in Britain finds that about 6.1 per cent of men and 3.4 per cent of women report having had a homosexual esperience in their lifetime, but only 1.1 per cent of men and 0.4 per cent of women report having had a homosexual partner in the past year. For many it is clearly a transitory experience, often a teenage phase, and unlikely to lead to permanent behaviour patterns (Wellings, Field, Johnson and Wadsworth, 1994:226).

Pressure groups argue that homosexuality is more widespread than it is, presumably to increase their ability to influence public debate. Certainly the presentation of homosexuality in the mass media is out of proportion to its numerical presence in the general population, and this has the effect of distorting perceptions as to its prevalence.

The causes of homosexuality are controversial. There are broadly two explanations: genetic and environmental. The genetic view is that a predisposition to homosexual behaviour or orientation is built in to the genetic make-up of the individual. Consequently homosexuality is fixed like hair or eye colour and must be accepted as a legitimate way of living. The environmental view of homosexuality is that it is caused by psychological factors in childhood or upbringing. The male homosexual often comes from a home with a weak or absent father and a dominant mother.

According to Moberly (1983) he looks for father love in an intimate relationship with someone of the same sex. Conversely, lesbianism, in the absence of a mother figure and in the presence of a domineering man in childhood, is explicable as a quest for mother love. The attraction, in these cases, between same sex people is not at first, or even basically, sexual but it takes on a sexual form because of the powerful sexual drives in adolescence.

If the environmental explanation is correct, we should anticipate, as a consequence of the general disruption of community life and the spread of previous unacceptable behaviour, a rise in the proportion of male homosexuals in years to come.

Counselling and cure

Bible-believing Christians are convinced that homosexual is sinful practice. They also argue that, since marriage is the only place where God has permitted sexual behaviour, homosexuals must remain celibate.

Homosexuals who come to Christian ministers for help want to feel they are understood. They may know the texts in Leviticus 18 that forbid homosexual acts and those in Romans 1:24f that depict homosexuality as the culmination of a process of spiritual decline. They wish to be accepted and not to be condemned or treated as worse than any other kind of sinner and some, like Pierson (1992), when they come to analyse the psychological forces that acted upon them in childhood and adolescence, learn to break out of their homosexual leanings.

Moberly (1983:24) points out that marriage is not the automatic cure for homosexuality. She diagnoses homosexuality as a form of 'immaturity or incomplete growth'. Same-sex needs must be fulfilled before opposite-sex needs (p 40), and this means that the normal cycle of human development must be passed through before maturity is reached. Same-sex needs should be met through 'corrective interpersonal experience' (p 42). Once the homosexual has learnt to relate to the same sex in a way that makes up the deficits that lead to homosexuality in the first place, the reorientation towards heterosexuality is ready to occur, but of itself marriage does not make up these deficits.

1 Corinthians 6 speaks of homosexuals in the Corinthian church who passed through powerful spiritual experiences. The process in verse 11 is briefly outlined: 'You were washed, you were sanctified, you

were justified in the name of our Lord Jesus Christ and by the Spirit of our God'. First comes faith in the atoning sacrifice of Christ, and this leads to justification. After this all the habits of thought and behaviour are cleaned by the action of the Holy Spirit in the new believer's life.

If the counsellor is faced with transvestites (people who want to wear the clothing of the opposite sex) or other sexual preferences, it is important to look for medical help. In addition guidance must be given concerning behaviour in church services. If you are uncertain about how to deal with this whole area, consult a senior minister or specialist counsellor.

References

Moberly, E.R. (1983), *Homosexuality: a New Christian Ethic*, Cambridge: James Clarke and Co.

Pierson, L. (1992), *Sex and You,* Eastbourne: Kingsway Publications.

Wellings, K., Field, J., Johnson, A.M. and Wadsworth, J. (1994), *Sexual Behaviour in Britain*, Harmondsworth: Penguin.

Chapter 17

CONCLUSION

There are numerous problems people might consult the Christian counsellor about, too many to enumerate here. When faced with a new problem we recommend that ministers look at the beginning of Part 2 of this book and use the information there to work out for themselves a Christian way forward. They may also need to consider the moral implications of the problem they face. What is right and wrong and how can the counsellee be encouraged to do what is right?

We would suggest that apprehension of right and wrong stem from the will of God. For the Christian the right thing to do is always the will of God. And the will of God is expressed through divine principles and commands given in the bible. In the modern world, however, there are issues that the Scripture does not directly tackle – these are issues that have only appeared since the time when the bible was written. For example, should a childless couple undergo fertility treatment? Should a Christian go on strike if a trade union calls one? The bible speaks about the blessing of children (Ps 128) and about the evils of injustice (Amos 5). On the other hand the bible shows childless couples praying for children (Gen 30:22; 1 Sam 1) and John the Baptist telling soldiers to be content with their wages (Luke 3:14).

In working out the right course of action the Christian must look for the essential features of the modern and biblical situations. The more similar the two situations, the easier it is to apply biblical principles. But there is a further set of considerations that may be brought into play because, in addition to looking for principles to be acted upon regardless of consequences, there is also a need to try to work out the probable benefits of a line of action. Which action will cause most good in the long run? We must try to calculate this, but often it is not possible, which is why acting according to principles can be simpler.

Finally, with regard to the kind of counselling a minister might carry out as preparation for marriage, baptism or Christian service, we recommend clear and positive biblical teaching that addresses the kinds of difficulties we have discussed in the counselling section and in the chapters on the minister's call and the cost of ministry. Our aim throughout this book has been to bring biblical truth into the practical and fast-changing everyday world.

Appendix 1:

THE WEDDING SERVICE

1. Wedding arrangements

a Meet the couple before agreeing to marry them.

b Ask them to attend a preparatory course on marriage; if you give the course, you may wish to cover the points raised in our section on marriage since an awareness of possible difficulties enables couples to organise their lives to avoid friction.

c On your final meeting give details of everything to do with the wedding procedure.

d Ask the couple to go to the Registry Office at least two months before they want to get married. If they are from two different registration areas, then both Registrars need to be contacted. This will cost them twice as much. The Registry Office will display a notice for 22 days announcing the intended wedding and, at the end of that time, will provide a blue form which *must* be given to the officiating minister. The minister is not allowed to conduct the wedding without the blue form. The blue form is valid for three months from the day that the couple first informed the Registrar of their intention to marry.

e Rehearse the service with the couple, i.e. practise down at the church.

f Make sure the music, flowers and caretaking of the church are covered.

g Give the couple a choice of wedding service either using one of the standard denominational manuals or prayer books or by letting them write their own service.

2. Filling in the register

a   The Register of Marriages must be filled in. If you are an 'authorised person' you may do this. Otherwise it is the job of the Registrar or an 'authorised person' in your area.

b   If you wish to become an 'authorised person', you will need to apply to the Registry Office for the necessary documentation.

3. The service itself

a   Be on time (about an hour before the service is due to start).

b   If you are an 'authorised person' yourself make sure you have the documentation for the wedding. You must write up the Register after the wedding has taken place.

c   Be smart and use the occasion to reach the relatives with good will and the Gospel.

d   Don't let the service be longer than one hour, less if possible.

e   Remember that the wedding service has certain *legal sections* that cannot be altered. They are the following declarations (which must be made orally at the time by each party in the marriage):

Since 1 February 1997, the marriage ceremony provides for a more modern version of the prescribed words of declaration and contract. The choice of prescribed words now permitted are as follows:

Declaratory words

I do solemnly declare that I know not of any lawful impediment why I, AB, may not be joined in matrimony to CD

or

I declare that I know of no legal reason why I, AB, may not be joined in marriage to CD.

or

By replying 'I am' to the question, 'Are you, AB, free lawfully to marry CD?'

Contracting words

I call upon these persons here present to witness that I, AB, do take thee, CD, to be my lawful wedded wife (or husband).

or

I AB take you CD to be my wedded wife (or husband)

or

    I AB take thee CD to be my wedded wife (or husband)

f   Show in your sermon the importance of a Christian marriage. This is also a time when you can share the Gospel with the relatives.

4. Legal conditions relating to the premises that must be fulfilled

Registration of premises

The church premises should be:

a   certified as a place of religious worship and
b   registered for solemnisation of marriages.

Registration forms are obtainable from the Superintendent Registrar of the district and must be signed by twenty householders who are members of the congregation. A building registered for marriages must contain a safe or strong box where the Registers can be kept.

Place and time

The marriage must take place:

a   in the registered building specified in the Registrar's *Certificate for the Marriage*;
b   with the consent either of the minister, or of a trustee, or of a member of the oversight;
c   with the doors open and between the hours of 8 am and 6 pm.

Check with the Registrar that all these restrictions are still in force since various changes are possible now that many kinds of location for a wedding are allowed.

Witnesses

There must be present at least two witnesses, and either an official Registrar of the district or 'authorised person', i.e. a person (usually, but not necessarily the minister) authorised by the trustees of the registered building or by the oversight of the assembly (and certified by them and the Registrar) to be present at the solemnisation of marriage in the building. Information about the appointment and duties of an 'authorised person' can be obtained from the Registrar of the district.

If you are the 'authorised person' please check that the ages of the persons to be married have not changed between their visit to the District Registrar and the date upon which they are being married. If a birthday has fallen between these two dates, then the age of the person should be changed when entering the details into the Register and upon the marriage certificate.

In summary

- The Registrar must be informed at least three weeks in advance and issue the blue form.
- The Registrar or an 'authorised person' must be present at the wedding and fill in the Register.
- The building where the wedding is carried out must be registered.
- The correct legal wording must be used at the appropriate point in the service.

Appendix 2:

THE FUNERAL SERVICE

Funeral Costs

a   The cheapest funeral today would be for a hearse and one car only.
b   Remember every time the body is moved (e.g. from hospital to Chapel of Rest) it will cost you a fee.
c   Shop around for the best prices.
d   Church fees need to be added to the cost of the funeral. A minister's standard fee is variable depending on the denomination and the travel involved. It may be around £70.
e   In addition to the minister's fee received from the Funeral Director there are the costs incurred of an organist, caretaker, etc.

Details to attend to

The following steps should be taken *by the family* in order to deal with the arrangements for a funeral:

a   Obtain from a medical practitioner a *Medical Certificate of Cause of Death*.
b   Go to the Registry Office taking the *Medical Certificate of Cause of Death*. The Registrar will write this information in the Register and give certified copies of the information (commonly called the *Death Certificate*) to the informants. Several copies of the *Death Certificate* may be needed for dealing with insurance claims, Probate, bank and building society accounts, taxation, and the like. It is cheaper to purchase several *Death Certificates* immediately from the Registrar rather than to have copies made

later. The Registrar will issue a green slip allowing the undertaker to proceed with burial. This green slip will be handed on to the minister if the burial takes place in a church graveyard. If the burial takes place in a council cemetery, it is passed on to the cemetery authorities by the undertaker.

c   If the Registrar is unhappy about the cause of death (for instance if the death is caused by an industrial disease), then the coroner will be called in and a post-mortem examination will take place.

d   Contact an undertaker. Do not necessarily accept the services of the first undertaker you contact. The funeral will cost anything from about £1000 upwards.

e   Notify distant relatives.

f   Notify the minister who will conduct the funeral service.

g   Notify the place of employment of the deceased person.

h   Notify the DHSS (you will need to fill a form in here). If the family is very poor, there is provision for about £500 to be paid towards funeral costs.

i   Contact the local newspaper and place an announcement in it of the time of the funeral.

j   Begin to make arrangements for the funeral. The time of the funeral will have to be convenient to the family, the minister, the undertaker and the cemetery or crematorium authorities.

k   Remember the Death Certificate serves as evidence of death in any official notification.

Visit to the family

The following points should be noted when visiting the bereaved family.

a   Phone to make an appointment (remember the day after the death is generally the day they have to do the rounds of the Registry Office etc).

b   Pray at the beginning of your conversation.

c   Listen and let the bereaved talk about the deceased person.

d   They may want you to see the body.

e   Approach the subject of hymns only when you have had a good chat.

f   When you are listening try to pick out a few good points for your sermon at the funeral.

g   Read a comforting passage from the bible.

h   Pray before leaving.

i   It is a good point to remember not to stay too long on your first visit, half an hour at the outside is recommended.

Things you need to know about the funeral day

a   Be on time at the church. Sometimes the relatives may want you to go to the house first for a word of prayer.

b   Remember you take the lead in all things, i.e. you lead the funeral procession (make sure you don't walk too fast; wait for the okay from the funeral director).

c   When you reach the front of the church or crematorium, wait until everyone is in place before proceeding with the service.

d   Speak out clearly, give clear directions, i.e. 'We will stand to sing'; 'Please be seated', etc.

e   Keep the service to about 45 minutes in church and 15 minutes in a crematorium. Crematorium services tend to run on an hour rota, please remember you have to be out within the half hour.

f   After the benediction take your place before the coffin to lead the mourners out.

g   Position around the open grave: the minister stands at the head, the immediate family at the graveside and friends a little further back.

h   Comfort and shake everyone's hand after the service. Be aware of the opportunity to share the love of Jesus at this point.

i   The position is the same for cremation, only the committal is different. The curtains are closed on the coffin as you say the words of committal. This is done in one of the following three ways:

1. By pressing a button that does it automatically.
2. By pulling a cord.
3. By the Director of the Crematorium when he hears you give the committal.

NOTE: It is not essential to draw the curtains.

j   It is always a good idea to go to the cemetery or crematorium before you have to take the funeral and get to know the Director and see how things are done. It might even be good to sit in a funeral or cremation service to see how other ministers do it.

k   After leaving the crematorium/cemetery you may be invited back to the house for sandwiches and tea. This can prove to be very helpful also in extending goodwill and the love of Christ to the wider community.

l   It is a good thing to visit the relatives again about a week later when everyone has gone back home. Bereavement takes a long time to come to terms with.

Additional notes

a   There are special words of committal for an unconverted person.

b   The best thing to do when taking the service of an unconverted person is to address the bereaved with positive help for them rather than to get into an embarrassing position of having to say he/she has gone to hell. It is also good to talk about the person who has died in positive terms with regards to their work, their interests, and their family relationships.

c   If you do not want to accept the fee then tell the Funeral Director there is no charge when he phones you first of all, or receive the money and give it to the relatives unopened after the committal. Always tell the relatives if you are not taking the fee to prevent the funeral director automatically adding it to his costs and then retaining it.

In summary

*   Take the *Medical Certificate of Cause of Death* to the Registrar and obtain the *Death Certificate* and a green form.
*   Take the green form to the undertaker.
*   Ensure that the date for the funeral is convenient to, and known by, the cemetery or graveyard authorities, the family, the minister and the undertaker.
*   Give proof of death to those who need to know by showing or sending the *Death Certificate.*

Index

Johnson, A.M., 180, 182, 183, 185
Jones, S.H., 44, 51, 63, 64, 70, 76, 168, 174
Jung, C.G., 138, 139

Kaldor, P., 7, 9, 93–99
Kay, W.K., 5, 8, 9, 94, 99, 103–106,
108, 109, 112, 113, 120, 122, 129, 133
Kerbey, A., 109, 112, 113
Kilner, J.F., 161
Kroeger, O., 143, 155

Lane Fox, R., 38, 51
Leadership, 17, 57, 59, 60, 62, 79, 81,
82, 85, 87, 88, 99, 127, 128
Letters, 70, 131
Lewis, C.S., 166
Life insurance, 16, 72
Liturgy, 35
Lone parents, 105, 106, 183–184
Luther, M., 12

Marriage, 15, 16, 46, 72, 97, 143, 144,
147, 152, 178–181, 184, 188–192
Masochism, 180
MBTI, 142, 143, 150, 178
McCaulley, M.H., 143, 155
McLeod, J. 141, 155
McGee, G.B., 9
Meeks, W.A., 126, 133
Meier P.D., 147, 148, 150, 154, 155
Messiah, 13, 116
Myers, I.B., 143, 154
Milner, P., 137, 150, 155
Minirth, F.B., 147, 148, 150, 155
Mission, 13, 37, 80, 89, 108–111
Moberly, E.R., 184, 185
Moody, D.L., 44
Mosaic law, 55, 116
Moses, 13, 30, 54, 89, 116, 130, 131
Müller, G., 30, 60
Murray, C., 6, 9, 15, 18
Music, 6, 8, 56, 85, 91, 107, 110–112,
125, 142, 189
Myers, I.B., 142, 143, 150, 154, 155

Naboth, 130
New birth (see Born again)

Newcomers, 96, 99

O'Collins, G., 130, 133
O'Donovan, O., 18, 155
Oil, healing, 41, 42
Old Testament, 13, 40, 54, 72, 119, 130,
152
One parent families, (see Lone parents)
Ordination, 15, 121
Oswald, I., 70, 76
Oxford Youth Works, 111

Palmer, S., 137, 150, 155
Pastors, 8, 22, 38, 40, 41–44, 47–49, 50,
59, 60–64, 70, 84, 85, 93, 95, 112,
144, 157
Paul, St., 13, 14, 17, 22, 23, 26, 30, 32,
37, 41, 45–47, 55, 56, 61, 80, 81, 88,
89, 98, 99, 116, 119, 131, 152, 168
Pensions, 72, 117, 178
Personality, 56, 70, 94, 139, 141, 142,
144, 145, 148, 155, 180
Peter, St., 13, 14
Phone calls, 25, 68, 69, 70
Pierson, L., 184, 185
Planning, 3, 30, 46, 61, 69, 81, 87–89,
127, 129, 142, 143, 164, 178
Political correctness, 29, 181
Population, 3, 4, 8, 40, 104, 129, 183
Powell, R., 9, 99
Prayer, 15, 16, 22, 25, 32, 35, 37, 41, 42,
44, 45, 48, 58, 60, 63, 64, 74, 88, 89,
94, 96, 110, 118, 148, 149, 151, 160,
168, 189, 195
Preaching, 13, 14, 22, 23, 27, 29, 31, 32,
35, 40, 43–46, 48, 53, 62, 69, 74, 80,
83, 89, 94–96, 111, 112, 121, 151,
152, 158
Presbyteries, 38
Prophets, 36, 39, 61, 62, 84, 118

Rahe, R.T., 143, 154
Ratcliff, D.E., 147, 148, 150, 155
Registrar, 189, 190–194, 196
Registry Office, 189, 190, 193, 194
Responsibility, 8, 28, 36, 48, 55, 60, 61,
67, 68, 71, 73, 75, 91, 95, 121